Politics of Purpose

The Centre for the Study of Democracy's (CSD) Library of Political Leadership

One of the first questions to ask about any leader is what are his or her priorities and do they run with or against the grain of history? An essential way of determining this is to research the public record and then compare dreams versus accomplishments. It is the public record of measured words that remains the most reliable barometer of either consistency or change in one's purpose. As Lord Acton wrote to the contributors to the Cambridge Modern History Project, "archives are meant to be explored". And because the written word is the key to describing ruling currents and interpreting sovereign forces, "we must provide a copious, accurate, and well-digested catalogue of authorities". To understand a public figure like John Turner, it is necessary to start with what he said and what he wrote. This is the founding volume in the CSD's Library of Political Leadership, an occasional series of collections of the public addresses of Canadian Prime Ministers, Premiers, opposition politicians and significant foreign leaders in the Canadian context.

Thomas S. Axworthy
Chair, Centre for the Study of Democracy
Library of Political Leadership Series General Editor

Front cover photo: JNT on the Burnside River, NWT, courtesy Geills M. Turner.
Back cover photo: courtesy Ian MacAlpine, *Kingston Whig-Standard*.

Politics of Purpose

40TH ANNIVERSARY EDITION

The Right Honourable John N. Turner,
17th Prime Minister of Canada

Introduction by Thomas S. Axworthy
Elizabeth McIninch and Arthur Milnes, Editors
Featuring photographs by Geills M. Turner

Volume I in the Queen's Centre for the Study of Democracy
Library of Political Leadership Occasional Series
Thomas S. Axworthy, Series General Editor
School of Policy Studies, Queen's University
McGill-Queen's University Press
Montreal & Kingston • London • Ithaca

Copyright © 2009 School of Policy Studies, Queen's University at Kingston, Canada

SCHOOL OF Queen's
Policy Studies

Publications Unit

Policy Studies Building

138 Union Street

Kingston, ON, Canada

K7L 3N6

www.queensu.ca/sps/

All rights reserved. The use of any part of this publication for reproduction, transmission in any form or by any means (electronic, mechanical, photocopying, recording or otherwise), or storage in a retrieval system without the prior written consent of the publisher—or, in case of photocopying or other reprographic copying, a license from the Canadian Copyright Licensing Agency—is an infringement of the copyright law. Enquiries concerning reproduction should be sent to the School of Policy Studies at the address above.

Library and Archives Canada Cataloguing in Publication

Turner, John N., 1929-

Politics of purpose / edited by Elizabeth McIninch and Arthur Milnes.

-- 40th anniversary ed.

Originally publ., 1968, in a bilingual format; this new edition includes additionalspeeches.

ISBN 978-1-55339-224-8 (bound). -- ISBN 978-1-55339-227-9 (pbk.)

1. Canada--Economic conditions--1945-. 2. Canada--Politics and government--1935-. 3. Canada--Social conditions. I. McIninch, Elizabeth II. Milnes, Arthur. III. Queen's University (Kingston, Ont.). School of Policy Studies IV. Title.

FC626.T87.T87 2008   971.064   C2008-903909-2

Table of Contents

Acknowledgements   VI

Introduction: The Pilot Who Weathered the Storm   IX
Thomas S. Axworthy

Chapter 1   1
Liberalism: Formula for the Future in the Past and Present

Chapter 2   23
The Political System: Re-shaping the Tools

Chapter 3   35
A Call to Conscience

Chapter 4   61
The Reformer at Justice

Chapter 5   101
The Canadian Identity

Chapter 6   115
John Turner's Federalism

Chapter 7   137
The Fight for Canada

Chapter 8   153
The Free Trade Battle

Chapter 9   167
John Turner in Winter: 1990 to Present Day

Acknowledgments

This book would not have been possible without the generous financial support of The Empire Life Insurance Company, The Dominion of Canada General Insurance Company, and E-L Financial Corporation Limited. Special thanks to Julie Tompkins, Director, Corporate Communications and Ombudsman at Empire Life for her assistance.

James C. Temerty, Chairman of Northland Power, made a substantial contribution to Queen's University in order to help the university honour his friend, Canada's 17th Prime Minister through a conference. We gratefuly acknowledge his support.

The Right Honourable John N. Turner and Mrs. Geills M. Turner also assisted by opening up speech files, responding to telephone or email inquiries, and in particular, Mrs. Turner, a renowned professional photographer, now retired, graciously mined her collection of Turner family personal photographs at short notice.

Turner's loyal assistant at Miller-Thomson, Jill Hamblin, was very helpful as well. Marc Kealey, a former assistant to the 17th prime minister, supported this project in ways too numerous to mention fully.

At the Queen's University Centre for the Study of Democracy, Chair Thomas S. Axworthy immediately put his name and the Centre behind the project and wrote an introductory essay about Turner that brought this volume together. The Centre's coordinator, Julie Burch, also gave support that was above and beyond the call of duty. Mark Howes, Publications Coordinator of the School of Policy Studies and his assistant Valerie Jarus who oversaw publication of this volume merits a special thanks from Dr. Axworthy and the co-editors themselves. Queen's University Vice Principal (Advancement) David Mitchell, himself a noted political historian, was very supportive, as was Mr. Paul Banfield, University Archivist and his team at Kathleen Ryan Hall. Another proud Queen's man, media lawyer Brian MacLeod Rogers, whose great-uncle was legendary Liberal cabinet minister and Queen's Rector, Norman McLeod Rogers, generously donated his expert legal services. Sean Conway, also a Queen's graduate and current senior advisor to the Principal of Queen's, merits our thanks. Veteran *Kingston Whig-Standard* photographer Ian MacAlpine, who covered the

1984 Liberal leadership convention, allowed us to reproduce his photographs which appear on the back cover and in the Introduction. A special thanks to Donna Blanchet of Kingston Business Services and freelancer Melissa Leggett.

In Ottawa, Parliamentary Librarian William R. Young and his staff responded to numerous requests with their usual speed, efficiency and enthusiasm, as did Maureen Hoogenraad of the Political and Social Heritage Division of Library and Archives Canada (LAC), Steven Artelle, Manager, LAC Forum on Canadian Democracy and Grace Hyam, now retired from LAC. Kingston and the Islands MP Peter Milliken, Speaker of the House of Commons and his staff, including Heather Bradley and Colette Dery, were also of great assistance.

In Toronto, Doug Pepper, President of McClelland and Stewart was supportive as well. The editors acknowledge the hard work of 40 years ago by (now) Senators Jerry Grafstein, David Smith and the Hon. Lloyd Axworthy for their work on the original *Politics of Purpose*.

The new leader of the Liberal party, John Napier Turner, now Prime Minister-designate, and his family, David Turner, Andrew Turner, Elizabeth Turner, Michael Turner, Geills M. Turner receiving congratulations from the outgoing Prime Minister Pierre Elliott Trudeau, June 1984, Ottawa. Photo courtesy Ian MacAlpine, Kingston Whig-Standard.

The Pilot Who Weathered the Storm

As John Napier Turner approaches his eightieth year, the Centre for the Study of Democracy (CSD) at Queen's University thought it appropriate to publish a new edition of *Politics of Purpose*, a collection of speeches first produced in 1968, prior to the Liberal Leadership Convention. This revised edition contains many of the original entries, but also brings the public record of Turner up to date, with his post-1968 reflections on Parliament, government, the Liberal party, law, environment and history. Most importantly, documented here is the fight of his life against the 1988 Free Trade Agreement with the United States.

One of the first questions to ask about any leader is "What are his or her priorities, and do they run with or against the grain of history?" An essential way of determining this is to research the public record and then to compare dreams versus accomplishments. We live in the age of tattle-tale history, with biographers keen to pry into the private lives of their subjects and so-called friends who are too often happy to dish the dirt as long as the interviews are unattributed. But it is the public record of measured words that remains the most reliable barometer of either consistency or change in one's purpose. As Lord Acton wrote to the contributors to the Cambridge Modern History Project, "archives are meant to be explored". And because the written word is the key to describing ruling currents and interpreting sovereign forces, "we must provide a copious, accurate, and well-digested catalogue of authorities."[1]

"Politics," wrote Max Weber, is the "slow boring of tough boards." To understand a public figure such as Turner, it is necessary to start with what he said and what he wrote. What do we learn about the career and purposes of the 17th prime minister by reviewing a selection of his public addresses from the past 40 years? To many, the contents of this volume will have an old-fashioned, or an even anachronistic ring to them: Parliament, public service, duty, the rule of law, and love of country are the values which animate this collection. Compare and contrast the modern political

---

[1] Lord Acton, "Letter to the Contributors to the Cambridge Modern History Project," *The Varieties of History*, edited by Fritz Stern, New York, The World Publishing Company, 1964: pp. 247–249.

lexicon—*spin, interest, wedge issues,* and *animating the base.* Turner was born in an age where the old political virtues of character and commitment were still uppermost. He held true to those virtues, even as the institutions of party, government, Parliament, and media were changing all around him. He is a transitional figure between the more genteel age of King, Saint-Laurent, and Pearson, and our own hyperventilating political era of twenty-four hour news coverage, negative advertising, political consultants, Ottawa lobbyists, and increasing disdain for the current way politics is played by ever-greater numbers of Canadians.

Turner was born in London on 7 June 1929; the first child of Leonard Turner, an Englishman, and Phyllis Gregory from Rossland, British Columbia.[2] His father died when John was three and his mother, who had met Leonard Turner while she studied for her PhD. in Economics at the London School of Economics, moved the family to Rossland, BC. With his sister, the experience of being raised by a single mother profoundly impacted him. He was left with a life-long respect for women who worked and also raised their children.

Phyllis Gregory later moved to Ottawa, and became the most senior woman in the Canadian public service. Thus Turner grew up in the golden age of the Canadian civil service mandarins. Norman Robertson and Lester Pearson were friends of his mother's, as was R. B. Bennett, the Conservative prime minister. As a boy, Turner himself would occasionally meet Mackenzie King while walking his dog in Ottawa. Historian Jack Granatstein writes that the mandarins "were an extraordinary group of civil servants who collectively had great influence and power... and whose overall influence and impact were positive in the extreme."[3]

As a minister, Turner received extraordinary loyalty from his civil servants and he knew how to harness the brilliance of difficult men like Simon Reisman, the deputy minister of Finance. Turner valued the intelligence, dedication, and independence of the civil service. He once told me that he believed both in public service and *in* the public service. He also knew that as a politician, he had to set direction; it was his job as a Parliamentarian to listen to public opinion, to engage

---

[2] The details of Turner's career up to 1984 are well documented in Jack Cahill's *John Turner: The Long Run*, Toronto, McClelland & Stewart, 1984.
[3] J. L. Granatstein, *The Ottawa Men*, Toronto, Oxford University Press, 1982: p. xi.

it, and to educate it. In the Ottawa era of the mandarins, public policy combined both the memory and expertise of the public service with the energy and sensitive antennae of the politician.

Turner wanted these boundaries respected; more than once, in not too subtle a fashion, he told me that his department was not to be bothered by the "junior G-men of the PMO." If he felt that the Trudeau PMO was becoming too intrusive, that we were overstepping our bounds, we can only imagine what he thinks of the Harper Government, where every ministerial communication must be vetted centrally, where civil servants are kept on the shortest of leashes, and where ministers are not even allowed to answer questions about their own departments in Question Period. Turner's personal staff as minister included such aides as Sandra Kaiser, who helped ensure that his was one of the most professional offices in Ottawa, in part because he delineated so clearly the distinction between political and public service roles. Turner was not Prime Minister long enough to reform the machinery of government, but had he been given a mandate, the relentless growth in centralized executive power would surely have been stopped in its tracks.

Phyllis Turner eventually met Frank Ross, one of the dollar-a-year industrialists who went to Ottawa to help with the war effort. They married in 1945 and the Turner family moved to Vancouver. Ross eventually became Lieutenant Governor of British Columbia and had his own wide network of political and corporate leaders to complement the public service network of his wife's. Turner enrolled in the University of British Columbia where he studied politics under noted Professor Henry Angus. He wrote for the student newspaper, *The Ubyssey*, and excelled in track and field. He won a Rhodes Scholarship at UBC and was voted "Most Popular Student" by the school newspaper. He developed a distinctive style at UBC that stayed with him for the rest of his life. He had multiple interests, but particularly thrived in the company of jocks. He developed a slightly hilarious "rat-a-tat" jive-talking style that was captured and parodied perfectly by Christina McCall in a *Maclean's* profile in 1971.[4]

Turner may have loved Parliament and honoured senior civil servants (two unusual traits for a rebellious man in the 1960s), but he was certainly fun to be around; he always had an air of west coast informality about him. In his Liberal Leadership

[4] Christina McCall, *"Turner: The Once and Future Contender,"* Maclean's, May 1971: pp. 23–7.

campaign in 1968, his major pillars of solid support came from British Columbia and the Young Liberals. Keith Mitchell, Mike Hunter, John Swift, and Shaun Sullivan laughed, organized, and endlessly tutored me as a Prairie boy that British Columbia was a Pacific region, never to be lumped into the homogenous "West." Few MPs supported his 1968 run, but two of them were Ron Basford from Vancouver Centre, and Bud Orange from the Northwest Territories. They appreciated Turner's understanding of the psyche of those not from central Canada. When he made the decision as prime minister to run in Vancouver Quadra in 1984, in a very real way, he was coming home.

After graduating from Oxford, Turner practised law in Montreal, eventually winning his first seat in Parliament in 1962. The Montreal community, and especially his young contemporaries in the Quebec Bar, became a third pillar of influence, deepening Turner's knowledge of the different faces of Canada. He argued cases against such well-known Quebec lawyers as Jerome Choquette, Claude Wagner, and Philip Casgrain. He was even noticed by Premier Maurice Duplessis, who would take Turner to see the Montreal Canadiens play. In 1960, Turner delivered a paper on legal aid to the fabled Liberal party Kingston Conference at Queen's University. Almost inevitably, Turner began to move in Liberal circles, guided by John deB. Payne, Jim Robb, and John Claxton—all well-established members of the Anglophone community. Most importantly, his successful campaign in St. Lawrence–St. George introduced him to Geills Kilgour, a systems engineer with IBM, whom he later married. She, in fact, introduced in that campaign the first ever computer analysis of a constituency in Canadian history.

It was in Montreal that Turner developed his great love for the Liberal party. Unlike Jean Chrétien, his liberal roots did not go back generations.[5] John deB. Payne saw the Liberal party as an essential instrument of national reconciliation—educating English-speaking Canadians about Quebec and recruiting French-speaking Canadians to employ their talents in Ottawa. Within that larger mission, the Anglophones of Montreal were a key hinge in opening the Liberal party to talent. In the 1960s, Turner was the latest and most exciting representative of that long Anglophone-Montreal tradition.

---

[5] Wellie Chrétien, a paper mill machinist, served as a Liberal party organizer in Shawinigan and Wellie Chrétien's father, in turn, had been mayor of a nearby village for thirty years. See Jean Chrétien, *My Years as Prime Minister*, Toronto, Alford A. Knopf, 2007: pp. 14–15.

Turner has been a Member of Parliament from constituencies in Montreal, Ottawa, and Vancouver. Few leaders of Canadian parties have known the country as well. In addition to these three foundational experiences associated with these communities, a fourth influence on Turner's sense of purpose must be highlighted—his faith. This may be the most important element of them all. In May 2003, St. Jerome's University in Waterloo, Ontario held a conference called "The Hidden Pierre Trudeau" which examined the spirituality of the recently deceased leader. The keynote address was given by Turner and he intrigued the crowd with stories of how he and Trudeau attended mass together and shared a strong faith. "The Christian faith," Turner said, was one reason that Trudeau "felt that politics had to reach out to the wider good, the common good."[6] So it was, too, with Turner. He went to St. Patrick's College in Ottawa, run by the Oblate Fathers. Turner was an altar boy and can discuss the framework of St. Thomas Aquinas as easily as he can recall the track times of Roger Bannister. Influenced by the social encyclicals of the church, Turner told his biographer: "the social conscience inside me comes from a lot of those theological writings. I have an intellectual conviction to Catholicism and certainly all the habits of my life are Catholic. So the intellectual commitment accords with the emotional commitment."[7]

All four of these pillars of Turner's early life are currently under great stress. We live in a secular age where organized religion is finding it difficult to attract new recruits. The great public service of which his mother was part, and the institution of Parliament which so inspired him, have both been weakened by a too-aggressive executive. The ethos of the Anglo-business elite, into which his mother married, is no more, with Canadian corporate leaders eager to sell to the highest foreign bidder. The Liberal party's traditional French-English reconciliation mission has grown more difficult, as large numbers of French-speaking Quebecers have opted instead for the Parti Quebecois, or their federal cousins, the Bloc Quebecois.

Turner's world has been irrevocably altered. Many would argue that this is a good thing. The old Anglo-mandarin-Liberal elite was male-dominated (Turner's mother being one of few women in it), had almost no minorities, and was conventional—or even conservative

---

[6] The Right Honourable John N. Turner, "Faith and Politics," in *The Hidden Pierre Elliott Trudeau*, edited by John English, Richard Gwyn and P. Whitney Lackenbauer, Ottawa, Novalis, 2004: p. 111.

[7] Turner, quoted in Cahill: p. 43.

—in its morality.[8] But this was also the generation that won the war, built the cities, promoted mass higher education, invited millions of immigrants to our shores, and invented the welfare state. And all of this was done with a civility and generosity which would astonish onlookers of Parliament today. Old-fashioned, maybe, but the generation of Turner's formative youth built the decent Canada which has endured.

So, Turner's values can be readily gleaned from the public record that is contained in this volume. And yet, leadership is not only about commitment; it is also about character. Senator Alan Simpson, in introducing Gerald Ford to a Harvard audience, put it well: "If you have integrity, nothing else matters. If you don't have integrity, nothing else matters." I am not an intimate of Turner's. I supported him in the 1968 Liberal Leadership race, but I have never been part of his close circle, unlike my brother, Lloyd, who was a member of his staff. But I have admired him since we first met in the 1960s and I have seen him often enough in the subsequent forty years to gain some insight into his character.

Turner succeeded in his studies through hard work, good friendships, and by listening to mentors throughout his career. He never forgot those who tried to help him when he was young. (This past June, I attended his annual 195 Club birthday celebration in Toronto, and was pleased to see so many from younger generations turn out to honour their own mentor, Turner himself). John Grace, the former editor of *The Ottawa Journal*, would often tell me about the Turner he knew at St. Patrick's, years before he came to know the wealth that his mother's second husband brought to the family. Working as a volunteer on Turner's behalf in 1968, I met his friends from St. Patrick's College, including John Grace, Turner's friends from UBC, and his friends from Saint Lawrence-Saint George—all volunteering to help a man who had never forgotten them. After 1968, the legendary 195 Club, which stayed with Turner until the last Liberal ballot was cast, were equally loyal in subsequent contests.

Loyalty doesn't just come about; it is earned. Though one of the busiest ministers in Ottawa, Turner's door was always open for me when I went calling to do graduate research. He would listen to my complaints, agreed to meet my friends, and above all, respectfully

---

[8] Three books that describe this era well are Granatstein, *The Ottawa Men*, Toronto, Oxford University Press, 1982; John Porter, *The Vertical Mosaic*, Toronto, University of Toronto Press, 1965; and Reginald Whitaker, *The Government Party*, Toronto, University of Toronto Press, 1977.

listened to the views of a twenty-year-old. Once, while I waited in his outer office, I was surprised to see a group of Conservative MPs march out, laughing and full of good cheer. I asked Turner what they were doing there. "I always invite the opposition Members on Parliamentary committees to discuss my legislation in private," he told me. "They often have good ideas, and it makes it easier when I have to appear before the Committee." A generation later, he was still practising that ethic. On 3 May, 1989, when he announced his resignation as Liberal Leader, he told the House of Commons:

> I always tell my colleagues... be careful, respect others, we must respect the other members of whatever party because everyone here, each and every one of us, represents Canadians as a result of an election in a highly free country. This is and remains the forum of the nation.

Turner reached the summit of Canadian politics by becoming prime minister, though only briefly. He had had a golden career in Canadian politics, rarely making a mistake, before his resignation in 1975. But his return to active politics in 1984 was rocky. "A week is a long time in politics," said Prime Minister Harold Wilson of Great Britain, and Turner had been away for nearly eight years. In the 1984 television debate, Brian Mulroney clearly bested him; a proud man leading a proud party was reduced to forty seats, only ten ahead of the NDP. As the 1988 election approached, the media ceded victory to Brian Mulroney and said the real question was whether Ed Broadbent's NDP would replace Turner's Liberals as the Official Opposition.

One man, though, made a difference. Turner turned the situation around on the old-fashioned idea that election campaigns are about issues and platforms, not personalities and polls. He had read every paragraph of the 1,407 page Free Trade Agreement that Mulroney's government had signed with the United States. Defeating that agreement, he said, was "the cause of my life." Waving the agreement before crowds in community halls, school gymnasiums, and church basements, Turner ignited Canadians. In the French and English television debates on 24–25 October 1988, he marginalized Ed Broadbent and confronted Brian Mulroney. The last 15 minutes of the English language debate was the best performance of Mr. Turner's career. Those 15 minutes saved the Liberal party.

Turner did not win the 1988 election. His debate performance, however, briefly moved the Liberals into the lead. This, in turn, galvanized the Conservatives and the business community, who spent millions of dollars in advertising to "bomb the bridge" of Mr. Turner's credibility. The Conservatives won a majority, and the Free Trade Agreement became law. But Turner doubled the number of Liberal seats and it was clear that if the Conservatives stumbled, it would be the Liberals who profited. Speculation about the NDP replacing the Liberal party ceased. When Turner retired in 1990, the Liberals were poised to dominate the decade.

Turner's character is defined even more by his defeats than by his successes. He never gave up. In 1988, he soldiered on, nearly alone, despite a bad back. He never lost faith in the kind of Canada that had given him such an opportunity to shine. We will never know if he would have made a great prime minister; we do know that he was a great Liberal leader who remained true to the verities of one era, while trying to adapt to the demands of another. For the Liberal party, he was the pilot who weathered the storm.[9]

Thomas S. Axworthy

Thomas S. Axworthy is Chair of the Centre for the Study of Democracy at Queen's University in Kingston, Ontario. He was Principal Secretary for Prime Minister Pierre Trudeau from 1981–1984.

---

[9] George Canning used this phrase about William Pitt, the former British Prime Minister, to try and entice him to return to public life during the Napoleonic wars. See William Hague, *William Pitt: The Younger*, London, Harper Collins, 2004: p. 499.

Chapter 1

Liberalism: Formula for the Future in the Past and Present

"We wanted to change the world and that's why we were there," John Turner once said, referring to the Young Turks, as they were called, the talented young Liberals elected in June 1962 who were determined to rebuild the party their way. Boisterous and brainy, this flock of MPs was a tribute to a generation that believed in public service and the Parliamentary tradition, in dedication to country and the empowerment of people. Turner, himself, was a star in that firmament. The handsome, popular Turner was MP for the colourful Montreal riding of St. Lawrence–St. George; he would be appointed parliamentary secretary to Arthur Laing, the Minister of Northern Affairs and National Resources, at a time of intense, dramatic debate over the Columbia River Treaty and a time of fascinating discussion over the future of the Canadian north and its peoples.

Turner was a charismatic, restless presence in Canadian political life, and his proposals for change reflected the buoyant optimism of the sixties. For the reader of today, his speeches of this period show a deep sense of understanding of the country and its challenges many of which resonate powerfully as we debate the future of Canada in 2009. Stating that democracy was invisible in political organizations, he called for sweeping reforms of Parliament and for more power for individual Members of Parliament. As early as 1962, Turner was on the road, telling audiences that continentalism was "not part of his vocabulary." As we will see, he would become this country's pre-eminent advocate of a national resource policy.

He threw down the gauntlet to Canadians on the subjects of economic rights and political freedoms, of law reform, of power to the consumer, of corporate governance and the immense tragedy of poverty. Over the decades, his message remained remarkably consistent. Energized by the power of his liberal principles, he was one of the great social and political reformers of his time. We begin with some of his fine speeches on liberalism which were what helped define his politics of purpose—in short, his call to conscience.

The notion of openness as fundamental in the functioning of a healthy democracy was a central premise in Turner's speeches over time. In the jaded, often cynical times we live in, his speech to the Canadian Bar Association annual meeting in Winnipeg in 1976, is a powerful message about the responsibility of citizens in the never ending struggle to build better democracies. His thoughts on restoring the party to the people in his speech given at the Halifax Reform Conference, November 1985 remain as astute today as they did then. Indeed, the timeless liberal values that anchor his speeches are a message of hope to Canadians of all generations across this vast land.

Elizabeth McIninch

A Second Canada – Prospects for Liberalism
From a Speech to the Western Canadian Young Liberal Policy Convention
25 February 1967 – Calgary, Alberta

Liberalism is not a dogma but an attitude of mind, and it is a state of mind that distinguishes the liberal from the conservative... What separates liberalism from conservatism is a difference in the flexibility of the human spirit. The conservative is suspicious of change; he adopts it reluctantly; he moves with an instinctive caution; and if he could, he would leave things the way they are—with improvements at times, perhaps, but basically the way they are.

A liberal, on the other hand, is a reformer; he has the zeal of reform; he is impatient with the imperfections of today and looks forward—eagerly—to a better tomorrow. This being so, the liberal has an openness of mind, a willingness to experiment. And make no mistake about it; this difference exists today in Canada between the Liberal party and the Conservative party. They can copy our program, but they can never steal our spirit.

No greater liberal ever lived in this country than Sir Wilfrid Laurier, and he put it this way:

> I am a liberal. I am one of those who think that everywhere, in human things, there are abuses to be reformed, new horizons to be opened up, and new forces to be developed.

The liberal is interested in people, not property. He is concerned with the personality of politics. He seeks the fulfillment of the aspirations of the individual in society. This, I should think, is what Mackenzie King meant when he said that the main concern of liberalism is with human well-being.

A liberal must be tolerant, because liberalism rests on faith in man and on the recognition of the worth and dignity of every individual. Indeed, is not faith in one's fellow man the very basis of democracy? Unless we believe that in most circumstances, over a period of time, the people, in their good collective common sense, usually arrive at the right conclusion. Unless we believe that—we do not believe in democracy. Democracy—government by the governed—depends for its essential validity on the assumption that those who are governed have the ability to judge those who govern them.

This is an assumption, in turn, that the people have been given the chance to judge, that the issues have been put squarely before them in understandable and communicable terms. We, as liberals, must not consider ourselves wiser than the people, because we are not. The people are entitled to know what we mean. In the words of Lester B. Pearson: "Liberalism, in contrast to hypocritical and cynical expediency, must always be grounded in honesty and responsibility and integrity, and in unshakeable belief in the dignity and worth and common sense of the individual..."

The art of politics, after all, is the guiding, directing, and controlling of the aspirations of human nature. A political party must be willing to undertake the risk of leadership and thereby the risk of defeat. We must take our chances with the people.

The time has arrived when Liberals must seek a new approach—not only in policy but in method. We must seek not only to criticize the other parties, but also to advance a positive program in fulfillment of new goals.

Here are my three challenges: one, we must seek a new approach to economic growth and full employment—a new planning; two, we must seek a new freedom for the individual in society; three, we must seek a new federalism, a new unity ...

The crucial issue in Canada today is that of economic growth and full employment. Once again I would submit that we must meet the challenge of change. To do so, liberalism must now accommodate itself to economic planning. By economic planning I do not mean socialist planning, whereby the instruments of production, investment, and distribution are absorbed by the state. I mean, rather, an economy whose direction is charted by government with the advice and with the free cooperation of management, labour, farmers, and other economic groups so that long-term and short-term goals can be set for this country...

This is not an anti-liberal idea. On the contrary, it is a liberal response to changing conditions. Is it opposed to private enterprise? I don't think so. Is the setting of goals contrary to private enterprise? Should the businessman object to this? Every business—large or small—plans, or should plan, for the future, and set targets for itself. Surely, then, the largest and most important business of all, the business that concerns us most intimately, the Government of Canada and her provinces, must plan. If government does not plan, no other business can...

In so striving, we could move forward toward a forecast economic growth—and more important, we could eliminate the most patent blights on our land, chronic poverty and unemployment. This waste of human resources, this affront to the dignity of so many men and women, this could be cured at its source. I commend, therefore, new planning—the first response of contemporary Liberalism to the challenge of a changing world...

There is a second frontier for Canadian liberalism to cross—I speak now of what I call the "new freedom." If liberalism has any criterion, it is its recognition of the worth and dignity of every individual.

We must rise to protect the individual citizen from all types of abuse inflicted on him. There are men and women whose rights are infringed on today because they do not have the bargaining power in life to protect themselves.

Consider the case of the individual caught in the machinery of government—that faceless superstructure which we have erected around ourselves. We must preserve the individual's right of appeal from the ever-widening discretionary and administrative powers of government. Not only should we protect the individual against bureaucracy, but also we should reform the internal workings of the machine itself... The areas where man deals with his fellow must be explored by a new spirit of business and big business. Why could we not create a new branch of the judicial system, for an ombudsman whose duty would be to intervene at any time on behalf of those who are being unfairly treated? ...

This is more than jargon. To my mind, it is essential for Canada that we reconcile the so-called "classic" federalism (and its division of legislative power into federal and provincial jurisdictions) with the modern economic necessity for national planning and central control of fiscal and monetary policy.

While this conflict involves the federal government and all the provinces, it concerns the province of Quebec most of all because of the fact of language and race... As liberally-minded Canadians, as reformers, we have to solve and bridge this philosophical—and psychological—gap. We must understand that there is, today, an evolution of ever quickening proportions in Quebec. It is up to us to recapture the allegiance of those who are intent on remolding Quebec. If separatism is to be beaten, if this argument in Quebec that

French Canada will remain a perpetual minority and can never fulfill its destiny as part of Canada is to be silenced, then it seems to me that two things must be done.

First of all, fiscal scope must be given to Quebec and to the other provinces to fulfill their legislative responsibilities. Quebec in particular must be made to feel that the destiny of French Canada can be accomplished within the present scope of the Canadian political framework. And secondly, the federal dialogue—the important conversation between French Canadians and the rest of Canada—must be re-established.

Let us not underestimate the importance of language, the medium of personal communication. In order to bridge the psychological gap between the two elements in our country, we must overcome the problem of language and promote a true bilingualism at the federal level.

I do not mean that we must achieve a bilingualism right across the country. That is obviously impractical. In Toronto, not everyone learns French, and if one does, it is not of necessity but as a cultural advantage. Nor [will an] act of Parliament change this. What I do mean is that wherever in Canada there are substantial numbers of French-speaking Canadians, the federal aspects of our national life ought to be open to them with all possible speed in their own language. Only in this way will French-Canada turn back to Ottawa.

There are many other issues to explore. The challenge of change must provoke the liberal to re-examine the world in which we live, to question the whole system of our society, and to look outward and around us, where on every side trade and political patterns are shifting. Everywhere people are on the move, and we in Canada—especially we Liberals—cannot afford to stand still.

If we meet this challenge, we shall be consecrating ourselves as a party of reformers, seeking the elimination of the abuses of today and answering the demands of a changing world in a dynamic, positive way.

Three Challenges for Contemporary Liberalism
From a Speech to the Alberta Liberal Association

17 November 1962 – Alberta

All around us today the danger warnings are out. Politicians are in disrepute. Parliament is low in public esteem...

There is a new generation of Canadians entering the arena of decision-making. This new generation demands a fresh, hard look at our political institutions—the party, Parliament, government, and the public service. How are decisions made? What are the reasons? What are the options? They have a concern that the Canadian political system is not fully meeting the demands of the contemporary age.

Liberals must meet this concern. We must search for, discuss, and indeed fight for policies and ideas of imagination and daring. I would like to tell you of some of my own personal concerns—where I think the Liberal party should be going in the future.

I am concerned, first of all, that we have not firmly established in our minds or hearts a Canadian identity. We need a vibrant, vital spirit. I believe there should be a spirit of nationalism. Not merely an emotional spirit which is fixed on the precedents of the past. I believe in nationalism, yes—but not a hard, narrow, and parochial nationalism which disregards the realities of the world and the diminishing dimensions of our globe. I believe in nationalism, yes—but not inward looking nationalism that fails to recognize the "global village" that has refashioned our lives. I believe in nationalism, yes—but not at the sacrifice of a minimum standard of well-being for all Canadians...

We must move forward in our search for a common destiny, guided by our collective conscience. We must have a reforming nationalism in Canada. We must have people who believe that there are pressing needs all about us, needs that we must face. We need people who believe that a social conscience is more important than a social consensus.

Enthusiasm is required. A responsive vehicle for reform is necessary. Our concept of government must be reassessed if we hope to carry out reform and change. The function of government must be defined. Government is a positive instrument. Just as there is an ever-increasing expansion of activity in the private sector of our country, so there is an expansion of government both in size and in its impact on our lives. Government in our modern, complex society must be efficient, and yet responsive and open to the opportunities of the future. The prime role of our federal government is to define our national goals. The federal government does not have a monopoly of wisdom. There are other forces in our society that must also shape our destiny. But the federal government, because of its central place in our society, must focus, crystallize, and define the goals we set for ourselves...

The tradition of the Liberal party holds that, when individual initiative and enterprise have not taken the necessary steps for material progress, government must intervene. Government does not necessarily begin new enterprises unless business and the private sector have not and will not undertake them for the public good. But about the growth of government we must be cautious. We must guard against conformity and regimentation. We must not create an uncontrollable leviathan. Modern government should be streamlined and efficient, but it should not in any way reduce the liberties of citizens, but rather increase them. In the Liberal party we are not afraid of government; yet we recognize its limitations. We must also recognize that reform can improve its role...

Let me turn to policies—policies to accelerate our entry into a second Canada. There has been a great debate in our party about the domination of foreign investment in our industries. This calls into question not only our relations with our neighbour to the south, but also our control of our economic destiny. This loss of control is a danger, and a pressing one. We must clearly know and determine what our national assets and our national resources are. "Continentalism," let me make clear, is not part of my political vocabulary.

Foreign investment and economic domination are a problem. But a greater problem of concern to Canadians is putting our own house in order. I am concerned that our economic institutions are held in too few hands here in Canada. I am concerned that our society is not an open society but a closed society. The upward mobility of our skills and talents is fraught with obstacles. Real opportunity to reach the pinnacles of our business institutions is foreclosed to many people. Opportunity in Canada is based less on ability than on background or social position... I am concerned about civil liberties in Canada. I am concerned that for over a hundred years we have not enshrined in our constitutional law a bill of rights. We pride ourselves on our tolerance, but this is a false pride. I am concerned that there are growing traces of intolerance and indifference in my country—intolerance of culture, intolerance of religion, and even intolerance of race. The second Canada must free itself of the prejudices which anchor it to the past.

I am concerned for the economic well-being of all Canadians. We talk of freedom, but we mean only political freedom. Freedom must receive an economic interpretation. We must provide a platform of economic security for all Canadians. The wealth of Canada is so great, and yet so unevenly shared. There are everywhere pockets of poverty, and inequalities between our urban and rural people. We must build a platform high enough so that the waves of economic fluctuation will not drown those who are on the periphery of society or who must maintain themselves on fixed incomes—the pensioners, the aged, the unorganized, and the mixed farmer. If we believe in freedom, we must ensure that the rich resources of our country and the wide range of our individual talents are not allocated to the extravagance of the few, while the basic needs of the many go unsatisfied. If we believe in this freedom and yet do not provide every Canadian with a minimum standard of well-being, we must re-examine our definitions and our programmes for freedom.

Liberalism has its roots in our diverse origins, in our two founding cultures. But many Canadians are descended from that segment of the Canadian population once called the "New Canadian" or immigrant society. Today the children and grandchildren of immigrants do not feel they are part of a minority. They feel proud of their origins, but do not yield to anyone in their sense of patriotism to this country. Our large metropolitan areas, such as Montreal (which I represent), or Toronto, or Winnipeg, and the West are peopled by those who came from the ends of the earth to find new opportunity and a new tolerance in Canada. Generations of men and women came here in hope. These men and women are a living example of the roots of the second Canada. They have given more than they have received. They have produced leaders. These are men and women who have worked with their hands and by their sweat. They have been driven by a yearning for an education for their children which they did not have the opportunity to obtain. In an open society, every generation must have a better chance than the last. If Canada is to grow and develop, our doors must be opened to people who are prepared to come to us with spirit and determination—people with skills, muscle, energy, and a willingness and ability to learn.

Our progress as a nation can be no swifter than our progress in education. Education is not a cost, but rather an investment in our intellectual capital. Our economic growth requires the maximum contribution from every Canadian. We look to the mind as our fundamental resource. A resource developed today provides riches for tomorrow... We must therefore triple our present effort if we are to compete in the international race for economic advancement. Our intellectual capital is as vital to us as our economic capital. The second Canada must go to school. There our past will be defined, and there our future will be widened beyond our expectations.

What role will Canada play in its second century of existence? We cannot compete in numbers, we cannot compete in terms of gross national product, and we cannot compete in military power. But we can compete in excellence: we can create a climate in Canada where quality is the password, where excellence is king. What we must build from our centenary to the twenty-first century, during the next twenty-five years, is a new state—a state of excellence...

I joined the Liberal party under the leadership of Lester B. Pearson because I believed that the Liberal party was the only true vehicle for social reform in Canada. I felt the Liberal party could bring to fruition my ideas and my concerns for Canada. Under Lester B. Pearson, we started once again down the road to the future. We have come a long way, but we have a greater distance to travel. We must trace the future with a bold, political breed of individual—not those who are stereotyped, static, or doctrinaire in their thinking. We need people who have open, dynamic, outward-looking minds and a vision of a second Canada. We must build, streamline, and galvanize the Liberal party as a political vehicle which, confident in its ability and conscious of its desires, can mould and shape the second Canada. The Liberal party must orient itself to the second Canada. If we do not, we do not deserve to be a political force in this country...

Our hope and faith, as Liberals, is that we can shape the forces of the future rather than have them shape us.

We cannot be proud as Liberals while there are students who have a desire to go to school and are not able to go. We cannot be proud as Liberals while there are people who are sick and are not able to get necessary care. We cannot be proud as Liberals when a decent home is not the birthright of every Canadian. We cannot be proud as Liberals while there is poverty in this land of plenty—a poverty which grates our conscience and blights our entire society. Unless we improve, unless we become better, unless we do more, we will not succeed—and history will point [an] accusing finger at us.

The Liberal program and Liberal policies must go down on the record of history, not as the ideas of one political party but rather as Canadian ideals and Canadian programmes. We are seeking in our party not a call to consensus, but a call to conscience—a call to elevate and share the conditions of our life here in Canada with our fellow citizens and with the world.

Freedom of Information
From a Speech given to the Canadian Bar Association Annual Meeting
30 August 1976 – Winnipeg, Manitoba

The strength of a democracy lies in the mutual confidence between those who govern and those who are governed. Information is the lifeblood of that confidence. Openness is fundamental to it. No democracy can work without an informed citizenry.

People must know what government is doing or trying to do if they are to hold government accountable, and make rational decisions about their own lives... but there is no way a citizen can participate unless he or she knows the facts and reasons upon which policy is based. Governments often complain that citizens do not understand what they are doing. Politicians feel that the remedy is more ministerial speeches, news releases and even an Information Canada. That doesn't work. The only cure is the facts.

It has been said that information is power. If that be so, to withhold information is to abuse power. Secrecy provokes myths, and creates tension and a lack of trust. Produce the facts and you dispel the myths. Produce the facts and you restore public confidence. Maxwell Cohen put it even more strongly:

> It is the degree, the timing, and the correlative disclosures that marks the difference between a "free" policy, and a silent tyranny, where secrecy stand as a high barrier to any public share in, or surveillance over, decisions and their makings.

In Canada, there is no legal right to know—nothing in the British North America Act, nor any other statute. Nor is there a legal duty on the government to inform. On the contrary, secrecy is sanctified by the *Official Secrets Act* and the civil servant's Oath of Office and Secrecy.

It is true that a Member of Parliament has question period and can file a Notice of Motion for Production of Papers. But the rules for production are established by the government. Production is discretionary, restrictive and reinforced by a majority. A good MP who uses these tools or remedies with skill and persistence can be quite effective, but the weight is still on the government's side...

Why do politicians and bureaucrats hold their cards so close to their vest? I suppose that one should make the initial observation that the appetite for secrecy is not the exclusive preserve of government. It is endemic to all large organizations—big business and big labour. There is the natural reluctance of the organization person not to be seen out on a limb. The more concealed the facts or reasons, the less likely that those in authority will have to admit mistakes...

Certainly, in politics there is a vested interest in presenting any policy or any decision in the most favorable light. This sometimes means selecting facts. It often means managing or manipulating information. It often involves orchestrating the timing. Full and immediate revelation of all facts can be embarrassing. I know—I've been there.

Politicians are not entirely to blame. Ultimately, one gets the type of government one deserves. Where people care, there is less temptation to be secretive. Government gets away with it because not enough people care. There are not too many Ralph Naders around. I happen to think that is too bad. I am glad The Canadian Bar Association has brought the issue of freedom of information before this convention. When I last spoke to our convention in Ottawa in 1969, I said that my thrust during my tenure in Justice would be a threefold one: first, to balance the rights of the citizen against the state; second, to give Canada a more contemporary criminal law—credible, enforceable, flexible, compassionate; third, to promote equality of treatment before the law for rich and poor alike.

Privacy and freedom of information fall under that first heading. And so did the new *Expropriation Act*, the *Statutory Instruments Act*, and the *Federal Court Act*. I wanted a freedom of information act. I stated to that convention that the public could not be expected to dialogue or meaningfully decide if it was refused the very information which would make dialogue and decision-making possible.

That need is even more acute now. We are long overdue for a freedom of information act in Canada. This convention should review the issue. We should not forget that it was only after ten years of pressure by the American Bar Association that the United States passed its own *Freedom of Information Act*. We may yet work wonders in Canada... ideas are contagious...

I have always believed that there ought to be a freedom of information act in Canada—one that takes into account the unique properties of our own system of government. We need a far-reaching statute which applies, not only to departments, but to agencies, tribunals, and crown corporations. We need a statute which imposes a legal duty on the government to make information available and which gives the citizen the corresponding legal right of access...

The exemptions... the first relates to the effectiveness of our cabinet system which operates on the principle of a collective executive and responsible government. It is essential to this principle of cabinet solidarity that neither the personal views of the ministers, nor any differences of opinions which precede a decision, become public. That pertains to the minutes of cabinet meetings or any other cabinet document containing advice or opinion...

While secrecy can be justified to protect the confidentiality of the advice, opinion or forecasts in cabinet documents, the decisions themselves and the facts in the documents (as opposed to the opinion) should be disclosed... The second sphere of exemptions involves information which could jeopardize the safety or security of the state and its relations with foreign countries. I am referring here to military and tactical secrets which could endanger defence or national security...

I do not, in this context, equate the economic well-being of the State with national security. In fact, I recall my first speech in the House of Commons was to demand that the then Minister of Finance, the late Mr. George Nowlan, produce the daily exchange figures during the dollar crisis in 1962. I had earlier accused Mr. Diefenbaker of having committed a fraud on the Canadian people for having concealed the figures. Ultimately the statistics were made available but not before "harm to the national interest" had been raised as an objection.

The third sphere of exemptions relates to information which the government acquires from members of the public. Seven years ago, I said that the right to privacy and the right to know are not contradictory but companion rights. I said that the right to privacy and the right to know are twin freedoms under a democratic order...

In contrast to the first and second spheres of exemption, which I would like to see narrowly drawn, the third category should have wide reach. Any information solicited from a person for one purpose which anyone, without that person's consent, seeks to use for any other purpose, should not be disclosed, unless the person seeking the information can establish that the public interest in disclosure overrides the private interest in confidentiality...

We are all aware how time-consuming and expensive a court action can be. But no forum is better suited or more familiar with balancing private and public interest, giving meaning to statutory language or deciding the application of exemptions. The court's role can be particularly valuable for the third sphere of exemptions, calling for adjustments between conflicting private rights... With respect to the other exemptions, cabinet confidences and national security, the court should also be the final arbiter by way of in camera proceedings. I must say, however, that this is a conclusion in which I come with some reticence, because I believe we should take care not to assign predominately political tasks to our judiciary...

Whatever legislation may be adopted, openness of government remains an attitude of mind. There may be no truly effective way to guarantee public access to information. There should be a statute. I believe the courts have a role... but I believe, as I said at the outset, that open government is a prerequisite to a healthy democracy.

Without it, there can be no participation or involvement. Without it, there will continue to be distrust. Openness is the beginning of an active citizenry, informed and, therefore, alert. Openness is the fount of trust in government because our elected representatives will become accountable not merely for the results or consequences of policy but for the reasons, the motives and the facts behind policy. Only in this way will government become fully responsive to the people who elect it.

From a Speech to the Liberal Leadership Convention
15 June 1984 – Ottawa, Ontario

You know—we all know—there are no easy solutions, no quick fixes. But whatever we do, however we do it, it will never be done at the expense of the unemployed, the poor, the aged, the sick or disabled. I believe in the Liberal heritage of the universality of our social programs. I want to lead this party so no future government of another political stripe will ever dismantle or tinker or destroy what we Liberals have built.

I am committed to economic equality for women. I believe in equal pay for work of equal value. That means affirmative action to remove the barriers that now prevent the recruitment and advancement of women. That means aggressive training and retraining programs to make them eligible for promotions and career options. That means adequate daycare facilities. We are not only going to change the law—more important, our leadership will influence a fundamental change in attitude. We will fight bias and prejudice. I will ensure that more women run for office in the next federal election. Women have helped set our agenda for a new era of issues. It is critical that women now be elected to public office so we can implement that agenda...

We are a country of minorities. Whether we speak English or French, we are Canadians first. No matter where we came from or how long we have been here, we are Canadians first. Canada loses as a nation if we do not take advantage of the unique and different backgrounds, skills and abilities of all our citizens. Equality in our country must become a state of mind. There must be total accessibility, free from discrimination and prejudice, for Canadians of every culture, into the mainstream of our national life.

Our country must have economic growth to do what we must and should—take care of our aged and our sick, create jobs for our unemployed and our young citizens.

Our economic and social objectives are complementary—not contradictory. I will continue to support the family farm, the most stable unit in agriculture. Young people must be encouraged to remain on the land—and farming must remain our most productive industry and allow us to feed a hungry world.

Canada is a trading nation. The international marketplace is in a state of flux. Competition is fierce. We no longer enjoy exclusive markets for our products.

This week we have our opportunity to reach out to our fellow citizens. We Liberals can say proudly that we have always been the party of reform, the agent of change, change that works for Canadians and not against Canadians. We have always formed the coalitions that banded Canadians together—not pandered to the powerful and the privileged. We have always welcomed dissent. We are at our best when we find common ground among opposing views. And now our party must become more open, more accessible, more accountable. When tomorrow is over we will emerge—as we always have—a united party, a party renewed.

I will repeat here a pledge I have made in every province of Canada. I will do everything in my power—by actions not words—to make the West a true partner in Confederation. If you give me your confidence and your trust tomorrow, I shall recruit men and women of quality and calibre—candidates who credibly represent the communities of Western Canada. Together we will win seats from the West…

There is a sense of urgency abroad in our land. This is no time for business as usual. It is a time for action and initiatives—you know it—and I know it. My friends, to implement our agenda I need your support tomorrow. I ask you to give me your vote. With your help we will rebuild the Liberal party as a truly national party from coast to coast, a new coalition of Liberals, a new confederation. We must earn their confidence by the strength of our actions in meeting their needs, of building their hopes and dreams…

I am anxious to help our Native peoples achieve a sense of self-reliance and a sense of autonomy. I am committed to ensuring the security of our elderly people. As a country we are ill-equipped in terms of research on aging and chronic care facilities. My vision of a new Canada is one where everyone participates, where everyone shares in a partnership between people, between regions and between governments. National unity, like equality, is also a state of mind, a set of attitudes. And in saying this I am thinking of this most gentle giant whose greatness of spirit was only exceeded by the size of his heart, the man who 22 years ago persuaded me to enter public life, the late Right Honourable Lester B. Pearson…

We are living through difficult times. We are faced with a world which is over-armed and underpaid. Too many weapons, but not enough bread. Too many walls, but not enough jobs. And our survival, our safety, our security depends on the active and constructive role which we must play in world affairs... But first and foremost we must devote all our energy to slowing down the arms race, the nuclear arms race. We all supported Prime Minister Trudeau when he moved forward, when he expressed his views on the world scene, and that work must be continued. The great tradition, the apostles of peace of the Liberal party must be continued. We shall try and find solutions for the conflicts. We shall help countries in need to build economies and to build their societies. There will be no tomorrow for Canada in a nuclear world. It will be my mission to see that we do our part to ensure that there will always be a tomorrow...

This has been a remarkable, eventful day... For Liberals in this great assembly and across Canada it is the beginning of an era of reform and renewal. For Canadians it will be the beginning of a new era where hope, confidence and compassion will be the guiding aims. Let us all rejoice in these new beginnings.

FROM A SPEECH IN HONOUR OF THE HONOURABLE JACK PICKERSGILL
20 JUNE 1985 – OTTAWA, ONTARIO

First of all, I want to say how very pleased I am that all of you were able to be here to help celebrate Jack Pickersgill's eightieth birthday.

As I look out on this group, I can see that we have in this room at this moment, probably the best and most representative collection of Liberals to be brought together for some time. In particular, I want to welcome Pierre Trudeau, who led this party with courage and foresight for so many years.

If Mackenzie King brought us from out of the caves of parochialism; and Louis St. Laurent moved us from the Middle Ages to modern times; and Lester Pearson led us into the wider world; Pierre Trudeau certainly presided over our "coming of age" as a full and equal partner on the international scene—and for that we will be forever grateful...

Tonight we honour a man who played a key role in the political life of our country and in our party for the past 50 years. I don't think Jack Pickersgill knew what he was getting into back in 1937 when he joined External Affairs as a foreign service officer, and when—

a few short months later—he was seconded to the office of Prime Minister Mackenzie King over in the East Block. The peaceful days of Oxford—with Jimmy Sinclair and others—were over.

You had a sparkling and exciting career—through the war years—and during the post-war period with Mackenzie King. I've always liked your description of the transition to St. Laurent. In your book, *My Years with Louis St. Laurent,* you say that King "handed me on to St. Laurent with the rest of the furniture." All I can say is—second hand maybe—but second rate never.

You were always ready to work out a strategy to solve a problem; always ready to offer advice and counsel. Joey Smallwood depended on that advice and counsel in bringing Newfoundland into Confederation in 1949. It is said that Joey Smallwood did two great things in his lifetime: one was bringing Newfoundland into Canada, and the second was bringing Jack Pickersgill into elective politics...

I got involved in the Liberal party in large part because I saw the ideas and the energy coming out of the Kingston Conference of 1960—the emphasis on rebuilding and renewing the apparatus of the party without abandoning the principles we share, the principle that the individual takes precedence over the state. Most of that energy and those ideas were coming from Jack Pickersgill.

And after we made it back into government, Mr. Pearson was kind enough to give me the job of Minister without Portfolio as a kind of understudy to Jack Pickersgill—then the Minister of Transport (and no friend of former Prime Minister John Diefenbaker). I think he was a bit disappointed when you left the House of Commons in 1967. He tried to cover it up though. I can see him now—those famous jowls, those piercing eyes, elbows flapping, head shaking—saying "Parliament without Pickersgill is like Hell without the Devil."

Once, while vacationing down south in the islands, I pulled Mr. Diefenbaker out of a dangerous undertow that was dragging out to sea. I have the awful feeling that to this very day Jack has never really forgiven me for that particular act!

You have walked through history with many great and lesser men. You have dedicated your life to the battles for social justice which have made this country what it is today—medicare, old age pensions. But the magic which is Jack Pickersgill is the openness of mind; the willingness to learn new facts; and to share that insight and knowledge freely—and to give so generously and so unselfishly of your time and your commitment.

The debt we owe you—as individuals, as a party, and as a country—can only be repaid with our simple gratitude—our simple thanks. The eightieth year is something special for anyone, but it is something very special for a man who embodies liberalism in his heart and soul—and has practised, spoken for, advocated, and fought for those ideals for over half a century.

FROM A SPEECH TO THE LIBERAL PARTY OF CANADA REFORM CONFERENCE 9 NOVEMBER 1985 – HALIFAX, NOVA SCOTIA

This is the first major national conference of a national political party ever to be held in Atlantic Canada. This conference represents phase one of the comeback of the Liberal party.

I have been here three times within the last year and what a difference a year does make. We have the honour of having attracted a good many of the national media, who came here for a number of purposes. Fourteen months ago we were consigned to the political trash can. We were dead. We were consigned to a footnote in history. Mark Twain was once accused in a newspaper in Tennessee of being dead and he had to reply in a letter to the Editor "rumours of my death have been greatly exaggerated..."

This has been a conference of process—how we do things. And those who observe how we conduct ourselves have said "what about the substance?" I say, to begin with, process is vital to democracy; it answers the question: how do we conduct ourselves? I don't deny that now we are going to need to answer what? and why? What do we stand for? Our policy. Policy renewal is already underway in every constituency in the country, riding by riding. It will culminate through regional conferences, provincial conferences, into a great national policy conference a year from now...

This is a time to rekindle our liberalism. In policy terms, now that we have the process of our procedures underway, it is time for us to examine why it is you and I are members of the Liberal party. Why do we call ourselves Liberals? It is the one political philosophy that has promoted an atmosphere of political freedom, of democratic capitalism, and of pluralism in our cultural and religious beliefs. And first of all, liberalism extols the supremacy of the individual and the rights of the individual over the rights of the state. Liberalism seeks to allow every individual to develop to the full limit of the law and the full limits of his or her potential. We believe in equality of opportunity, equality in terms of access to education, to jobs and training, and options, regardless of colour, creed, religion, region and family background.

Liberalism provides the widest possible scope for the individual and for the initiative of each of us. Liberalism rewards success. If you do well under our society, we believe you should be paid for it, and you should enjoy it. There is no politics of envy in the philosophy of liberalism. None! More power to you.

We also believe that we have a duty as a community to protect those who, for reasons beyond their control, are unable to protect themselves—the unemployed, the aged, the handicapped. Sure we believe in private enterprise, but we recognize that there is a positive role for government where private capital cannot do the job or where the public interest of the country demands it. We are not doctrinaire, we are not ideological, we are not rigid, we are not static—because the world is not static. We reject monopoly power, whether that power is exercised by business or by union or by a religious cult or even by a majority.

To paraphrase those great words of Sir Wilfrid Laurier, we accept change and we seek it. We believe in reform and we fashion it, and we believe most of all that human beings can improve themselves. We believe that the world can become a better place if only we try hard enough. We really do believe that it is perfectible.

This conference is ample proof that as a party we recognize the need to re-examine ourselves; to re-examine the way we are structured; to re-examine the way in which we conduct our business. But we do so in the knowledge that our basic principles such as I have attempted to recite them—our basic principles are sound and that we are on solid ground.

When we are re-thinking approaches we are not re-thinking our principles. We are designing here a mechanism to apply better those principles to the problems and opportunities we face as individuals and as a nation in the next generation. Keep in mind the words of Thomas Paine, "Moderation in temper is always a virtue—but moderation in principle is always a vice."

So now we are getting our own affairs better in order. I believe and see our challenge as a party is to firmly focus on the type of country we want in the year 2000.

First of all, I see a strong and independent nation. I see a strong and independent nation on the northern half of this continent beholden to no one but ourselves.

The word sovereignty is legalistic and juridical. But during the summer, when Geills and I picnicked and barbequed across the country, we found that the issue that disturbed Canadians most of all last summer was the fact that our great neighbour to the south had publicly and deliberately inserted a public American ship through waters that we believed were Canadian. They did not recognize them as Canadian and they did not have the courtesy to ask our permission, and our government did not have the guts to demand that they ask our permission to go through those waters.

We Canadians are a unique and vibrant and diverse culture. We have some respect in the world as a voice of moderation and a voice of common sense. But we are going to have to preserve our dignity as a nation by speaking out loudly, boldly, and proudly without hesitation...

This party, under Mr. Pearson, invented—prompted and provoked and prodded by Joey Smallwood—the theory that there should no longer be regional disparity in this country. I told Joey Smallwood, (I used to deliver messages between Mr. Pickersgill and Mr. Smallwood—(and) destroyed them immediately thereafter), I don't understand what regional disparity means, but I do understand what regional equality means. I know that there should be equality for every Canadian whether you were born in Cape Breton or Prince Edward Island or Newfoundland. You don't have to live in Toronto to get a good education and to get a job and to get fulfilment of your life. No way!

The Conservative Government is cutting back brutally. Cutting back brutally on the principle of regional equality. I said in the House of Commons last week that the government had cut the Atlantic provinces adrift. The same goes for Gaspé, the same goes for eastern Quebec, and the same goes for Northern Ontario and a good many parts of our western provinces. We are going to fight for and stand up for the principle of regional equality in this country... The family farm is in trouble and our fishermen are in trouble. I can't go into it more, but I tell you that we will not forget either the farmer or the fisherman in this country.

It is becoming clear that the party supposedly without a future a year ago is rapidly becoming the party that is going to shape the future of this country in a few years.

I can feel it. I think you can feel it. The renewal really is taking shape, taking form... This conference followed by our convention next year will give us an added burst of intellectual energy. We are going to need it. We are going to need it for the steady march back to giving this country the kind of good government it needs and deserves...

When you chose me to lead this party, your message to me was clear and unequivocal. You gave me the responsibility to lead the renewal and the regeneration and the rebuilding of a great national party and to implement once again the spirit of liberalism in our country. It is the biggest challenge in my life.

I have had the privilege of representing three provinces in the House of Commons. In the past eighteen months I have met more Liberals than anyone else in this room and I have listened... I have listened and I have told Liberals everywhere—don't be discouraged; we can come back. Canada is still a moderate, tolerant country. We are a progressive country. Canada is still a liberal country. It may be that over the years of power we grew more remote and we grew more distant, even more arrogant. Some of us may have felt that we have a divine right to govern. Some may have thought we have a vested interest in the administration of Canada. But the Canadian people wanted change and we were defeated. There are very few advantages to opposition, but there is one clear opportunity. Now we have the chance to renew ourselves in spirit, in people and in ideas. We have a chance to reach out, to rebuild and to rethink... The last sixteen months have given me immense, unlimited, affectionate confidence in the Liberal party and in you. Trust me. We will earn the confidence of Canadians once again soon. We are on our way back.

Chapter 2

The Political System: Re-shaping the Tools

Like William Lyon Mackenzie King, the most successful Liberal leader of them all, John Napier Turner served three different provinces as a Member of Parliament during his career. But unlike King, Turner was never defeated and forced to seek a quick by-election. He served the people of Quebec, Ontario and British Columbia over four different decades in Canadian public life, winning each and every riding election he contested.

As his political opponents would agree, Turner is a House of Commons man.

> I say this not in any pompous way, I hope, but I remind particularly our young Members of Parliament from all sides of the House that Mr. Diefenbaker used to say: "Don't neglect this place, spend your time here. It may take many years to build up a reputation in the House of Commons but you can lose it in one day."

That was the advice Turner gave the Commons after members from all parties paid tribute to him on 3 May 1989, when he announced his resignation as Liberal leader. He added:

> This is the highest court in the land. This is the place where finally issues must be decided... But the word Parliament, taken from the Norman, was well chosen. This is theatre, this is debate. It is the freest Chamber in the free world. It is unruly at times, but it is untrammelled and uncensored, and unpredictable.

When he first published *Politics of Purpose* in 1968, Turner embarked upon his literary journey, thanking MPs from all parties in the opening of his book. He wrote, "Despite public criticism—much of it justified—Parliament is still our greatest forum of democracy."

His beliefs remain as strong today. But on the matter of re-shaping the tools of government in a modern and complex democracy that is

Canada, Turner was and is a reformer. Unlike some who followed him, Turner never feared listening to opposing views in a parliamentary or political context, even those points with which he strongly disagreed on a personal level.

During his first speech to the Commons as Leader of the Opposition in the fall of 1984, he called for the election of the Speaker—something that became a reality after the McGrath Commission report prompting the Mulroney Government to accept this historic change. As Attorney General, Minister of Finance, and indeed in all the portfolios Turner held, he demanded more and more ideas from his political staff and a team of brilliant civil servants.

As Liberal leader, Turner returned the party to the people to whom it truly belonged: ordinary grassroots members in ridings from coast-to-coast-to-coast. And by doing so, he helped bring to the table new Canadians and others who had been shut out in the past.

In political retirement, the old reformer has remained true to his beliefs, sometimes shocking friend and foe alike. At one of his annual birthday gatherings at the famed 195 Club, he announced he was excited by the entry into a federal leadership race of neo-conservative Tom Long. But how could Turner, progressive Liberal he's always been, be excited that a man of Long's views had entered the public arena? Of course, Turner's remarks about Long were leaked to the media—as he surely knew they would be. More debate, more discussion. More voices to consider. That's Turner's approach.

"A crisis has never been avoided by silence," he wrote in 1968. And through debate among our parties, our government and our Parliament, we will indeed build a better Canada. The only bad idea, he would say, is one not debated.

Arthur Milnes

From a speech at McGill University
29 January 1964 – Montreal, Quebec

The Member of Parliament

The function of today's House of Commons is neither to legislate nor to administer. Government by public meeting is pretty well impossible. What happens in effect is that the Commons elects a business-like board—called the Cabinet—to govern the country, and then the Commons keeps an eye on the proceedings of the Cabinet. In fact, the House of Commons elects a prime minister, who selects his Cabinet; but thereafter, the House cannot control the everyday workings of administration.

There is a severe limitation on the power of the House of Commons: the practise of the collective responsibility of Cabinet. The Cabinet stands or falls as a unit. If a minister is challenged on a matter of government policy, the Cabinet stands behind him and will stand or fall with him. There is, therefore, always the threat to the Commons, by the Cabinet, of dissolution and an election. The Commons can challenge a minister for departmental incompetence and sometimes destroy him. But a minister who is departmentally responsible for a Cabinet decision cannot be pulled down in this way—unless the Commons is prepared to face the resignation of the whole Cabinet and the threat of an election. This means the government (meaning the Cabinet) is immune to Parliament, except on issues of crisis.

This is not to say that the Cabinet form of Government is inherently wrong: it is rather a necessary product of the urge for efficiency in the management of the business of the country. But the concept of the Cabinet reduces the role of the MP to that of expressing the grievances of the people. So, in a sense, the power of the House of Commons is a myth. In theory, the Commons can do anything; in practise, it can do little.

There are further restrictions on the role of the MP: party organization and party discipline. A century ago the private member was genuinely free to defy the party whip or disciplinary agent of his party. It was this independence of the ordinary MP that gave the House of Commons its importance—and was the best check upon the government of the day. Now, as Richard Crossman, the well-known Labour MP in England, writes, "the prime responsibility of the member is no longer to his conscience or to the elector, but to his party. Without accepting the discipline of the party he cannot be elected, and, if he defies that discipline, he risks political death."

What does this mean? It means, first of all, that the debates in the House of Commons, which used to make it the forum of the people, have become mere sounding boards. It means that there are no longer any surprises. It means that Cabinet, through the party, controls the private members who support it. Real struggles for power today are not fought on the floor of the House of Commons; they are fought inside the party councils. The caucus of the government party and of the chief opposition party have become the real battlefields of politics. Democracy has become invisible. How long can it remain invisible and hidden from public scrutiny and still remain a democracy?

Party discipline can easily be exaggerated. There is, in the conscience of every private Member of Parliament, a point where principle dictates that he must rebel against his party. This still happens, but not as much as it used to—and it is becoming harder to rebel. As the political party becomes more organized and more disciplined, the scope of the backbencher becomes more restricted.

There is, therefore, very little possibility of a surprise in the result of a debate. The government's majority is usually automatic, the decision is known before debate begins, and nothing anyone can say during course of debate can alter this. Admittedly, in these days of minority government, where no one party has a majority, there can be surprises in the ultimate result of a vote. But the fact that every member usually votes according to his party discipline means that the debates no longer mean what they used to mean. Debates have become largely a sham.

There may be those who think the debates are useless anyway, and that parliament ought to get on with the business of the country. Too much talk, not enough action. We should be careful about this type of argument because, to paraphrase Winston Churchill, democracy may not be the most efficient type of government we have, but it is the best system that man has yet devised. Efficiency, however, has its price: a corresponding loss of freedom. Dictatorship is more efficient than democracy—and every citizen has the choice of whether he wants to bargain his freedom for this type of efficiency. Talk is essential to democracy and the House of Commons is the forum of the nation. The point is, however, that the talk must mean something. That talk becomes meaningless if debate is not going to have any effect on the final vote—and these days the debate does not affect the vote, because the party caucuses have dictated the final result. The House of Commons becomes less of a place, if the results of the debate are determined beforehand.

Should we be against party discipline? No. Party discipline is necessary—without it there is incoherence in politics. The slogan, "Every voice—a vote," means ultimately chaos and anarchy, and leads to the type of government which befell the Third and Fourth French Republics. What has happened, however, is that the proper balance has been lost and party discipline has become too severe.

There are other forces that restrict the MP. We cannot ignore the power of the civil service, what has been called the "mandarin class"—the faceless experts, protected by the anonymity of a government department and operating beyond the range of the people's control. This is not an attack upon the civil service. We need an efficient civil service, which gives us the balance of efficiency against the freedom of an elected legislature. Democracy might flounder for a time because people may be confused (and the confusion will be reflected in the legislature), but if the civil service is strong, the government will run. But today the power of the civil service—the concept of efficiency—outweighs the impulse to freedom, as personified by the MP. We need an effective counterpoise to the civil service in the person of an effective MP. The average member is faced with a monopoly of information and technical competence which he cannot match. As governments increase their intervention in our society, with economic planning, five-year plans, and the like, and, as the technical background needed for intelligent criticism becomes more complicated, a Member of Parliament fights a losing battle with the civil service. We must restore the balance.

Television has added a new factor: the leadership cult. Because of television, we now have really a presidential type of government in Canada. We have the prime minister talking directly to the people, outside of Parliament. We have the Leader of the Opposition doing the same thing. From battles between individual Members of Parliament, we had battles between parties; now we have battles and elections between titans, between superman-like leaders. We have the leadership cult.

So this is your Member of Parliament: whipped by the discipline of the party machines; starved for information by the mandarin class; dwarfed by the Cabinet and by bigness, generally, in industry, labour, and communications; ignored in an age of summitry and the leadership cult.

Fortunately, there is much an energetic and capable MP can do to reverse this trend, even without reform. More fortunately, reforms are coming—reforms in the business procedures of the House of Commons that will streamline the House and eliminate the duplication in debate that was tolerated in an earlier age. But reforms must affect the role of the individual MP as well.

Backbenchers on the government side of the House should be given a greater share in the legislative process: their views should be taken into consideration prior to the drafting of legislation. What happens now is that once legislation is drafted and reaches the floor of the House in the form of a bill, the government party's prestige is at stake. Government members are forced to rally around the bill, whether they like its terms or not. Giving members an opportunity to criticize legislation, before it reaches final definition in words, will restore a good deal of influence to the private member. Since the party caucus has become the real political battleground, the remedy of giving a member more scope in caucus by giving him the right to criticize legislation there, means that he can be more effective in Parliament.

Insofar as a member's relationship with his own party is concerned, my suggestion is that the government stop treating every vote as a vote of confidence. Procedural matters and matters affecting the private morals or judgment of a member—such as the questions of capital punishment, nuclear arms, and so on—might well be left to a free vote. Naturally, most votes have to be treated as confidence votes; but enormous life could be brought back to the House of Commons if the members could occasionally follow their own opinions regardless of the party stand. In such circumstances, if the Government were defeated, the defeat would not necessarily mean a loss of prestige.

A suggestion which is meeting with more and more support is that the committee system in the House be expanded. By this is meant a procedure whereby legislation be submitted at an earlier stage to standing or special committees of the Commons for scrutiny by the members. This reform would have two main results. It would, first of all, allow the Member of Parliament access to the information which is now denied him; he would have the opportunity, as a committee member, to summon witnesses from the civil service and elsewhere for interrogation on the facts surrounding the legislation. The monopoly of information would thereby be broken. Secondly, the reform would allow the member sitting in committee to be considerably freer of his party's discipline; and he would, in consequence have the scope to use his own judgment and talents, and to be less restricted by commitments to partnership.

This question of enhancing the vote and influence of the MP is not merely an academic one for debate in scholarly journals. The Member of Parliament must play an effective role. He is the safeguard of the people against government bureaucracy, and bigness in general—against the centralizing of power and influence. If he is freed from the monopoly of information, and freed somewhat from party discipline, he will play a more useful role in Ottawa. He will be better equipped to use his judgment, and in doing so, he will be representing us better. If his is a worthy and useful life, democracy in Canada will flourish.

Managing the Public's Business
EXCERPTS FROM A SPEECH TO THE MONTREAL BOARD OF TRADE ASSOCIATES
19 OCTOBER 1966 – MONTREAL, QUEBEC

Just as society is changing, the concept of government in our society is changing—and indeed must change. It is time to re-examine the function of government and to decide what its proper role should be. Just as there is an ever-increasing expansion of activity in the private sector of our country, so there is an expansion of government, both of its size and of its actual impact on our lives.

To begin with, all political parties in all parts of our country have come to realize that government must provide economic security for all Canadians where the private sector has not, in its unplanned growth, provided such security. I believe that all parties have accepted that government is no longer merely a regulatory force or policeman in our community, but is instead a powerful promoter of society's welfare. In these days of increasing affluence, no government can evade the responsibility of ensuring minimum economic security for all its people. No doubt the methods and speed used to reach this goal will vary with the men in government and with the party in power. No doubt in the future, as in the past, there will be a careful cooperation of federal government and provincial government in translating our universal concern for the individual into practise.

But whether we are talking about social security, economic direction, or resource development, the Canadian public will no longer permit government to shelve good ideas, to let them gather dust, or to leave them as unexecuted blueprints for the future. Our people now demand a programme of priorities of the development, protection, and management of our human resources and limitless material resources.

To translate such general policies into responsive legislation is difficult. It is even more difficult to give the words in the legislation meaning, and to translate these policies into action... Mr. Justice Felix Frankfurter once wrote that humane and sensitive government is impossible without well-trained, disciplined, imaginative, modest, energetic, and devoted administrators. Modern government will need even better talent than that which business and the private sector now enlists. John Stuart Mill put the principle even more precisely when he wrote that "mediocrity ought not to be engaged in the affairs of state." The future will provoke a growing competition between government and business for the brains and talent of this country...

We need in this country a new spirit—a spirit among men who are prepared to join the public service and be responsive to a country's highest aspirations. Why should not businessmen, skilled in the new techniques, bring their talents to the government? Why can't there be a sharing of ideas and talent between business and government to the benefit of the entire country? Reforms demand creative minds. These minds must be recruited.

We want a team of public servants who are a restless and creative breed. It is not healthy for our country if our civil servants remain static and self-satisfied.

I do not believe that government should grow inexorably bigger for its own sake. We must fight to defeat Parkinson's Law of bureaucratic growth. This bureaucratic growth is a danger, but no more than that. I believe that government must be quick and immediate in its response to the needs of each individual that is touched by its activities.

The problem, of course, is change. The rapid change in our society causes government—recognizing change—to make institutional reforms. Often these reforms become obsolete even before they are implemented. We therefore must structure government with agencies and incentives to cope with change. I believe that creative tension and competition for the common good among the departments of government is healthy, if responsibly and appropriately applied...

It is true that the objectives of business differ from the objectives of government, but this should not prevent us from using the methodology and approach to problems which are similar. Government must adapt itself to modern management techniques. We must have a government which becomes increasingly confident in the use of modern techniques in its problem-solving matters...

The record of government will not, in the future, be measured merely by how much money it spends, but by how well it spends it and by the results achieved by the money spent. We in the Government and in Parliament, as well as the public, will have to re-orient ourselves for the new thinking...

Government must set an example to the private sector. It is clear that, even with new techniques and developments, ours is a government of men. The federal government must set an example as the nation's largest employer. There will be no room for deadweight in government. We must ensure that government is not slow in the service it gives to the public. Government must be designed to serve the public swiftly and effectively. The problem is not how big government becomes, but rather how responsive to the needs of the people it remains. The danger is not big government but insensitive government.

In the new horizon of government activity—in social welfare, housing, and educational assistance and research—the government already has the power to help or hurt every individual in every community. Not to use these powers efficiently and effectively to help people is to use these powers to hurt or hinder people. I believe that we must ensure that government moves to help our farmers, our cities, our labour force, and our aged and infirm, and must tackle with all its might the problem of poverty in our society. Franklin Roosevelt said in 1934 that, "if government does not do it, nobody else will or can." Governments must intervene in these areas, and business must understand and meet its own commitments. I am not so much for big government as for effective government—a government which represents all of the public interest, and not any particular sector.

The public service must be as efficient as private industry. Increased efficiency in the conduct of public business should be reflected in budgetary savings. Our resources should not be wasted on internal government administration—but should serve the public at the lowest cost. We should be able to achieve improvements in productivity per employee in the civil service. Personnel should be better trained and better supervised, with more effective organization and more efficient equipment. Government itself must become automated, and open to technology where it can benefit. There is an urgent need to keep remuneration for the public career employees on a reasonable parity with private enterprise. Pay for civil servants should be based on the degree of responsibility and on achievement. We must continually be on the march to improve the services to the public, and to develop a reservoir of modern managerial talent...

Government is not a name but a service. When we take it on ourselves to expand government, then we must ensure that it is done properly, reasonably, and creatively.

Nomination of The Speaker
FROM A SPEECH TO THE HOUSE OF COMMONS
5 NOVEMBER 1984 – OTTAWA, ONTARIO

I am very pleased to rise in my place today to second the nomination of the Right Honourable Prime Minister (Mr. Mulroney) of Mr. John Bosley as Speaker of this House. I might say, had circumstances been different, I would have preferred to move the motion than to second it. However, I understand what the people of Canada have said and accept that fully.

I am also very happy to see Mr. Stanley Knowles sitting at the table. He sits as an honorary member of this House. No doubt his wisdom and experience will be of immense assistance to the new Speaker particularly, and to all of us in this Chamber.

Without in any way derogating from the choice which I second today, it might be well for future Parliaments to consider what the unanimous report of the Special Committee on Standing Orders and Procedure recommended in the last Parliament, namely, the adoption of a new Standing Order which would provide for the election of the Speaker by secret ballot by all members of the House. That will be something for a future Parliament to consider. As I have said, that in no way derogates from our approval of the particular choice this morning.

Perhaps it is also appropriate on this Guy Fawkes Day, as we open Parliament and elect a Speaker, that we remember that democratic institutions have sometimes been under attack, the Mother of Parliaments, to a lesser extent in this country than in other parts of the free world. Recent events indicate to us what a precious and fragile thing democracy is (Indian Prime Minister Indira Gandhi had been assassinated on October 31). The Speaker represents this Commons as the embodiment of the will of the people. Protecting the rights and privileges of this House will be Mr. Bosley's primary concern and more important, defending the rights and privileges of its Members.

It is particularly important in this Parliament, with the large majority on the Government side—and I might say surrounding us—that the Speaker exercise special care and vigilance in the protection of the rights of Honourable Members and, might I say, the traditional rights of Her Majesty's Loyal and Official Opposition.

From a Speech upon the official unveiling of his portrait,
Parliament Hill
8 May 2001 – Ottawa, Ontario

Give these members a voice, let them speak their minds, let them speak their consciences and let them represent the interests of their constituents... I urge the members of this House from all sides to reclaim the dignity and independence that begat our system (and was) so much in evidence during the early years of our Confederation ... I urge again, as I did in 1964, that the whip be withdrawn from Members of Parliament except on the Throne Speech, on the budget, and I can say to the Prime Minister (Jean Chrétien) on matters of critical national policy... The greatest honour our fellow citizens can bestow upon a Canadian is election to this place, the House of Commons. Parliament is the forum of our nation. It is not just a legislative machine, it's a place for debate both here and in the Senate when the main issues of the day should be debated and resolved.

Chapter 3

A Call to Conscience

By 1965, John Turner was seen throughout Canada as a 'Kennedyesque' figure intent on building a Canadian Camelot. He had acquired a reputation as a man of principle and an advocate of sweeping changes in Canadian life and society; he joined the Liberal party, he often said, because he saw it as the vehicle for social reform in Canada. His speeches of the period challenged young people to channel their energy, their intellect, and their spirit of change into the political realm. In 1965, Turner was Parliamentary Secretary to the Minister of Northern Affairs and Natural Resources. He had developed a love of country that he shared with the Blair Frasers and the Bruce Hutchisons of his time. His dream for Canadian youth was to see them travel and work in the North. He lobbied for an Arctic peace corps to bring southerners the reality of these striking and lonely regions.

In a speech to the Ladies Guild of St. Andrew's and St. Paul's in Montreal, 1964, he moved his audience with the message that the way we treat our Aboriginal peoples will reflect the depth of our national conscience. Many of his speeches in this period were anchored in calls to raise awareness of the significant social problems and challenges to development of this most beautiful land, a land he had traveled many times publicly with his Minister, and privately with his wife, Geills.

As Canadians ponder the injustices of residential schools in 2009, it is important to note that close to 50 years ago, Turner was lamenting the fact that Aboriginal children were being herded into boarding schools and hostels far from their families. In his field notes from the period (written in October 1963, after a 13,000 kilometre tour of the North, see Library Archives Canada series MG26 Q1, Vol. 6) he wrote:

> The classrooms of the north do not reflect the Arctic surroundings, as books, posters, and all forms of teaching aides are as remote from depicting Inuit family life as though the school were in Toronto... in our earnest endeavours to teach the English language in our schools, to fit the child for Canadian society as a whole, we appear to have looked clear beyond the most important reality in his or her life—his identity with his home, his parents... the wonders of his own land.

In May 1965, Turner was part of the historic Laing mission to the Soviet North—the first western tour east of the Urals. The Laing team was fascinated by the remarkable construction techniques in the permafrost carried out by the Soviets, and Turner gave a number of speeches on his return comparing development in the Soviet and Canadian norths. He wrote in his field notes at the time:

> Canadians should be talking in terms of participation and cooperation (with the Soviets)—not merely in terms of co-existence. It is possible to have a dialogue of differences. While being committed to the western alliance, Canada may facilitate an accommodation between Russia and the US.

Turner was a passionate advocate of a national resource policy. He warned Canadians that water was fundamental to the future of the country and that urgent action was needed to protect this inheritance. Canada's water became the issue that brought him to the nation's consciousness. After his 1965 electoral victory in the Montreal riding of St. Lawrence–St. George in which he won one of the largest pluralities in Canada, Turner was appointed Minister without Portfolio with responsibility for Transport. In April 1967 he became Registrar General, and in December 1967 he became Canada's first Minister of Consumer and Corporate Affairs.

The creation of the Department of Consumer and Corporate Affairs—the first in the western world—was a tribute to Turner. As the history of the creation of the new department shows, he had unparalleled political skills in balancing the host of government, regional and corporate interests involved in the complex environment of the consumer of the day. Turner had a masterful ability to balance vision and caution in the interests of Canadians. But when conscience called, caution was put on the back burner. The war against the drug companies was applauded in the editorials of the period. So, too, were his impassioned speeches to advertisers, accountants, and corporate elites to put the interests of society first, profits second. Indeed, his speeches of the day were remarkable forerunners of today's focus on the need for good corporate governance. We have included his Economic Bill of Rights, revolutionary for the times, which placed him far to the left of many of his supporters.

Elizabeth McIninch

From a Speech to the Ladies' Guild of St. Andrew's and St. Paul's
14 April 1964 – Montreal, Quebec

I believe that our Aboriginal people must be allowed to develop and live as ordinary Canadian citizens and be treated under the ordinary provincial jurisdictions of this country. They must not forever be a nation apart. They can no longer remain as second class citizens— as wards of the federal government. They must develop as citizens having the same rights and bearing the same responsibilities as any other Canadian. This was the purpose for undertaking negotiations with the province of Quebec with respect to the Inuit in the north. If the Inuit are to mature, surely they must be emancipated one day from federal trusteeship just as all... Aboriginal peoples (in Canada) must, so that they can become ordinary citizens of this country.

There are obvious conditions to any transfer of administration and the federal government has at every stage of the negotiations insisted upon this. We have insisted upon certain guarantees before any transfer is made. The Inuit must be guaranteed that their cultural ties throughout the North would not be broken; that their language would be respected; that they would continue to enjoy at least the same standard of services that they are now receiving. In other words, it would have to be part of any agreement to be negotiated with the province of Quebec that the same rights and the same services be guaranteed to that northern people.

And finally, the Inuit themselves must be consulted. Any agreement, before it is made, would be submitted to them, explained to them, and any views they had would be taken into consideration before any final agreement was made. The Inuit would have full opportunity to exercise their democratic rights to be heard...

This land, barren, yet theirs, has a lot of magic to it. 'Nunatsiavut' is the Inuit name. It means 'beautiful land,' and yes, their homeland is indeed beautiful! In the winter, storms can blow up to vicious white-outs; but the blue sky of a summer day has an eerie grandeur—this is a grand, strange, massive, lonely land! There are thousands of miles of treeless tundra, a great desert of Precambrian rock—yet this is a land that casts a spell.

Who can tell why some experiences in life touch the imagination while others, sometimes considered more important, do not warm or light up our lives at all?

Someday the Inuit will write about this vast northern country. Perhaps someday we shall have more Inuit poets write about their land and they will sing out the magic of this land in a few words what other people try to do—and often fail—in many. And they will say some of it in words that those who are not their people can understand. Here, for the moment, are a few lines from a visitor that captured the spirit of the Canadian North for me:

> Who will live in this tall, brooding land!
> Where winter silence on a windless day
> Is soundlessness so unlike any other
> That the ear can stop what it's doing
> And listen
> To the deep ring of nothing
> Silence so everywhere
> It is like
> The sudden stopping of the world...
> A rough lovely land
> Open, yet secret!
> Biting into the heart
> So that when remembrance has become a dream
> A scar of love remains!
> As with all, beautiful, solitary,
> And desolate places.

(Mr. Turner here to described the living conditions, lack of sanitation, and abysmal health, birth/death rates of the time.)

Ladies, the average life expectancy of the residents of Nunatsiavut is 29 years; this tragic figure can be equated with the average life expectancy of the citizens of Red China...!

The disappearance of game made the continuation of the old life impossible... few Inuit can anymore get a decent living off the land... the land alone will no longer support them. One quarter of the Inuit are now on relief... but this is a short term solution.

On a positive note, I have seen the wonderful new Inuit cooperatives which have meant a pooling of efforts and profits. New industries are now in operation—such as commercial fishing, fur garment making, handicrafts, the beautiful arts of sculpture, print making... housing construction.

The Inuit people are used to sharing and caring for one another in mutual defence in a harsh climate... from the cooperative spirit, new community leaders are emerging! But the best known co-op is located in West Baffin Island at Cape Dorset and was founded only a few years ago in 1959. I predict this co-op will be famous internationally in time. The graphic arts and sculptures of this artistic center are uniquely beautiful.

And at Kuujjuaq (Fort Chimo, at the time), we are now seeing the development of the exciting new rage—the Arctic Owl, or the Ookpik which was discovered in time for the spectacular Philadelphia Trade Fair last fall. Indeed, as many of you know, the Ookpik is now Canada's international trade symbol and the annual production of such art has topped the one million dollar mark. The sheer volume of production has resulted in the formation, with the assistance of the Co-operative Union of Canada, of an independent marketing agency —the Canadian Arctic Producers Limited.

...(In spite of all the challenges they face, I believe the motto of our northern peoples will be) Never say die! I am encouraged to think that this will be the spirit of the Inuit all across the North. And that as they face with southern Canadians—all the uncertainty of the second half of the 20th century—their spirit, the spirit of Nunatsiavut—the Beautiful Land—will never die.

That is my hope for our Inuit people, the majestic inhabitants of a land that has touched my heart and soul as no other.

> Editors' Note: The reader will note that the speech above was given decades before the creation of Nunavut on 1 April 1999. At the time, Turner was referring to northern reaches far larger than Canada's newest territory. He used speaking notes sketched on index cards and much of his presentation was probably extemporaneous. We have framed the excerpts above in speech format and have updated the language of the day to contemporary usage. Space allows us only a minimal look at the full scope of his thinking, but it was clear that Turner's very deep sensitivity to the challenges of the North, along with his visionary thinking (which was far ahead of his time), began to evolve in the early sixties, and engendered a lifelong process of commitment to the region and its peoples.

The Power of Youth
FROM A SPEECH GIVEN TO THE STUDENT SOCIETY OF MCGILL UNIVERSITY
29 SEPTEMBER 1967 – MONTREAL, QUEBEC

All roads now lead to the university: government, business, and culture are increasingly dependent on the choices made in the ivy halls. Innovation is the keynote today, and the resources of knowledge must be tapped, or else this society will grind to a halt. Increasingly, all of us live in a society shaped by our colleges and universities: they are really, as *Life* calls them, "Chart-makers for our Demanding Future..."

The real importance of young people today, however, is not their influence on popular culture, taste, or fashion. Young people are important because they are in the front lines of a battle to make the modern world liveable for individual human beings. The protest groups, the sit-ins, the reaching out for new forms of self expression—these are all signs to me that young people, at least, are attempting to resolve some of the glaring contradictions that exist in their world. The extremes of poverty in the midst of affluence, the co-existence of justice and injustice, and the paradox of mass-oppression in a society dedicated to liberty are the nagging sores that give rise to youth on the march.

Nowhere is this more apparent than in the community of the young, the university. We have seen in this country of late a powerful current of dissatisfaction among university students against the governing administrations of higher education... The voice of the young people is a voice which speaks for many in the wider community who sense a loss of meaning in old values, hypocrisy in present practises, and an irrelevance of many of our major institutions.

"The student grab for university power," as the *Globe and Mail* calls it, is an important assertion of the rights of individuals to be responsible for the direction and purpose of their own community.

And let me say that I welcome and applaud this refreshing challenge to authority, this drive for greater responsibility, this pursuit of new ideas and the ambition to restore a sense of individual present. In this battle, young Canadians carry the banner of a new generation that wants a different and better kind of world.

But what kind of world? I still see missing from those banners proclaiming youth-power a clear blueprint of where young people want to go. It is not sufficient to tear down old values if there is nothing to replace them. It is wrong to ask for more power if there are only vague indications of how that power is to be used...

Power must be balanced by responsibility, for the young as well as for the old. Responsibility does not end the moment one leaves the stage with a diploma in hand: if students want to make decisions they must remember that results of those decisions remain after they have gone. If they are to assume responsibility in the university community, then they cannot drop out after four years. There must be a continuing and lasting involvement in the life of an institution —a constant, life-long sense of obligation—a community membership that continues even after they have left the physical surroundings. Without this, their demands for power—only while as students—are licence for part-time stewardship and an abdication of obligation.

Let me also express one note of personal regret on the question of young people and their influence. There has been a powerful energy unleashed by young people. There has been a sense of exploration, a searching for new means to restructure this nation.

But all these efforts have by-passed our existing political system. The power of youth has not been felt in our political parties. I find young people treating our existing institutions with disdain or, even worse, indifference...

The tragedy is that our political system is exactly where young people should be. It is in the political arena where the critical choices of this nation must be made. It is through the process of political completion, conflict, and compromise that this country must hammer out the decisions of what kind of society we want to be. We live in a highly political age and we have a desperate need for new standards of idealism and morality.

The serious question of national unity, the momentous challenges of war and peace, the preservation of national identity, the eradication of poverty, the response to the scientific revolution, the urban chaos—all these are issues that, at the present time, are being grappled with inside political arenas across this country. They are live, vital problems in which daily decisions must be made. And decisions are being made without benefit of the kind of exuberance, dissent, and freshness that Canadian young people could contribute.

Think of the momentous task before Canadians at this moment. We must find new patterns through which the strands of national unity can be woven. The very essence of the Canadian nation—its capacity to house different cultures under one roof—is being eaten away.

I want to hear the voice of young Canadians on this issue. We hear the agitation of the separatists. But where are the spokesmen for those young Canadians who want to build a Canadian nation, and not to divide it? Where is the experimentation, the search for new ideas, the dialogue over alternatives by our young people?

This is not an issue in the abstract, but a concrete one that concerns every responsible political figure. This is the Canadian issue. It floods though every channel of our body politic. It desperately requires the attention, intellect, audacity, and honesty of youth.

There is a lot of elasticity in our parties—a great deal of room for growth. Our parties are like half-inflated tires, simply needing a good strong breath of fresh air to fill them out and let them do the job.

The fact is that political parties become ineffective only if sincere and critical people refuse the challenge of changing them. Our young Canadians must channel their energy, their intellect, and their spirit of change into our political realm...

The purpose of this generation should be a renaissance in politics. Young people have the real responsibility to change our political parties from simply election-day machinery into viable community organizations providing easy access for the ordinary citizen. There is the need to redress and restore Parliament. Our public service must be a more efficient instrument, better able to respond to contemporary demands. Most important, there is a need to search out and explore the philosophical underpinnings for new political debate and discourse. The greatest handicap to a strong, vital political system is that we are weighed down with ideological trappings that confuse our debate and becloud reality. A fresh dose of definition and dialogue is required to fuel our political machine. We must restore our political credibility, build better forms of government institutions, and create a new Canadian democracy. The new power of youth can find no better use of its muscle than to help achieve these ends.

Water: A Canadian Resource

From a speech to the Electrical Club of Montreal

3 November 1965 – Montreal, Quebec

It is my view that Canada at the moment does not have a national water policy. There is insufficient coordination between the federal and provincial governments in the formulation of a unified water policy. Not only is there little coordination between the federal and provincial governments, there is still too little coordination within the federal government itself. The federal government should set up a Canadian Water Authority, coordinating all agencies and uses within the federal jurisdiction and having the authority to formulate national policy in cooperation with provincial governments.

Canada is not yet prepared to think in terms of a continental water policy whereby we negotiate the sharing of the water of North America with the United States. We first must establish a Canadian water policy. Before Canada can contemplate export or sale of water to the US by way of diversion of our rivers or the creation of new water basins and canals, certain conditions precedent would have to be satisfied...

The establishment of a Canadian national water policy whereby we coordinate the federal and provincial administration of water use and establish our priorities over the various uses of water; The taking of a complete inventory on a national scale of our water resources; The preparation of an analysis of projected Canadian water needs into the foreseeable future so as to protect Canadian growth potential; The making of an analysis of the cost-benefit ratio to Canada of a continental water policy. How much would it cost? What would its benefits be? How much is it worth to the United States? How much should Canada charge for it? Enforcement by treaty of controls on international water basins, i.e., quotas and limits of how much water each side can take out of international systems—no drains without plugs.

Only when these conditions have been satisfied will Canada be in a position to negotiate with the United States. American thirst for our water will put tremendous pressure on Canada. We must therefore accelerate all the steps listed above and convert our analysis of water into a national priority. Unless Canada has this information we will not have the necessary equipment with which to maintain our bargaining position with the US. We will not know whether to sell, how much to sell, or what to charge. When we do start to bargain, Canada should insist that as water is considered as a continental resource, markets should also be considered on the same continental basis. The bargaining should therefore not be limited to the amount of financial payment by the US as under the Columbia River Treaty, but it should extend as well to opening markets to Canada in return for the sale of our water...

There are very few industries which do not use water in quantity and there are likewise very few industries which do not have wastes to dispose of. Water is a very convenient carrier of waste products and waste disposal is one of the most important uses of water. Every stream has a natural ability to cleanse itself when it is given a load of waste to carry. But there is a limit, and on many of our streams that limit has been reached... We in Canada have fortunately not yet reached the condition described by President Johnson, in a recent message to Congress, when he said "every major river system is now polluted," but we are not far behind, and I think it would be safe to say that every major river system in the settled part of Canada is polluted to some extent.

Is there any solution? Our industries and cities must dispose of waste materials. There is no question about it. But must we accept polluted streams as a corollary? I think not. Our scientists and engineers can tell us how to clean up our streams, perhaps not to the state they were in a hundred years ago, but at least to a state which would not impair our health or offend our senses... Resources know no boundaries. Pollution cannot be quarantined; it is contagious. It flows from one province to another. The federal government must not merely act as a referee; it must now act as a coordinator and must, on behalf of the people of Canada, bring provincial governments together by initiative and persuasion into coordinated national policies.

Test of Revolution

FROM A SPEECH TO THE UNIVERSITY CLUB
23 MARCH 1969 – VANCOUVER, BRITISH COLUMBIA

Just as much as we are citizens of Canada, we must be citizens of the world. Just as much as Canadians seek responsible leadership at home, they must be assured of a leader who gives them the guarantee of a firm, but responsible, hand abroad. Our foreign policy is a concern as vital to all Canadians as the problems of national unity, the problems of housing, of economic stability, of all the issues that affect the comfort and security of every Canadian...

I am here with only one purpose... to tell you where John Turner stands... This is an age of revolution—the revolution in time and space, which makes this world so interdependent, national upon nation... Then there is the most powerful of revolutions: the liberated force of human aspiration now sweeping the southern continents of the world: Africa, and Asia, and Latin America... in today's world there is no 'far away.' Can we think of Asia as far away, when we ourselves are a nation on the Pacific rim? I believe it is time we re-examined our geography. For too long Canadians have been mesmerized by the European, North American, Atlantic triangle. Yet the centre of world interest and world activity has shifted to the Pacific rim... yet Canadian foreign policy has been slow in reacting to the Pacific challenge... The Pacific rim is still a "no man's land" for most Canadians...

I spoke earlier of the revolution of human aspirations and the way in which it escalates to a revolution of arms. Surely this is what we are seeing in that tragic little country, Vietnam. A conflict spawned by many years of hunger, of deprivation, and loss of pride. The grinding pressure of an iron fist—and while the first may change, the pressure does not.

I sympathize with the American dilemma... the world power exercising its responsibility. I know, too, the almost imperceptible steps which have brought us, over twenty years, to the current situation in southeast Asia... I know that the only step which counts today is the step which is taken today. And in Vietnam, that vital step must be to end the conflict. American force will not solve Vietnam.

The force of a great power solves only a global war... and its use at any other time only invites that awesome possibility.

Here is where John Turner stands on Vietnam: step one, a halt to the bombing; step two, an explicit proposal, a spelled out proposal, of the eventual political arrangements. Such a proposal is to accept, to accommodate the genuine force of nationalism in Vietnam; step three, an eventual guarantee, a guarantee to all the nations of the world, of a state of neutrality for the whole of the Indochina peninsula. This neutrality under the auspices of an international body, and I suggest its composition be drawn from the Asian members of the United Nations.

Where does Canada fit into this? In two dynamic ways: one, we must take it upon ourselves to maintain an open channel of communication with both sides, perhaps by an expansion of the role of the International Control Commission. We must be known, and labeled and recognized as one of those intermediary nations, constantly arguing with both sides against escalation, and hopefully, for moderation.

Our second dynamic contribution? We must reach out an effective, realistic, helping hand to the people of Vietnam. Their needs are human... and we should meet those needs with an international plan of refugee assistance, reconstruction, and medical aid...

Revolution is spawned by tension and turmoil, which in turn are born out of basic economic and social problems... External aid can be increased both in amount and quality... our external aid is not charity, it is investment. Unless we invest in the developing nations, the gap between rich and poor will only grow wider, the stability will only increase. And we all will suffer. We must give the developing nations more access to the markets of the industrialized nations, more effective ways of selling their produce. We must revise the present trade patterns which now benefit only the rich states. In short, we must put aside our eloquent good wishes and replace them with real help.

The Troubled Consumer

EXCERPTS FROM A SPEECH GIVEN TO THE OTTAWA CARLETON LIBERAL ASSOCIATION

15 NOVEMBER 1967 – OTTAWA, ONTARIO

Across this country there exists a large body of Canadians who are separated from the main cluster of their neighbours. We rarely see them. They rarely demonstrate or protest or make themselves visible. They are those whom Michael Harrington, in his book *Other America*, called "the hidden poor"—the outcasts of an affluent society.

I became vividly aware of this separate nation with the assumption of my new responsibilities for consumer affairs. I see them as members of a large group of "troubled consumers," those, who in our modern marketplace, have special needs and special circumstances: There are the elderly on fixed income, caught between rising costs and the difficulty in gaining full medical attention, proper nutrition and decent housing services; there is the small farmer whose land is not sufficient to supply his family and who must rely on high-cost credit to finance improvements; and the urban worker faced with expensive modern metropolitan demands, but with a job which doesn't provide enough money. These people add up to a large number of Canadians who have been by-passed in the forward pace of our progress. There are too many Canadians who still live in poverty, who have been left behind the main thrust towards advancement and opportunity.

Poverty, in contemporary Canadian terms, is a condition of not being able to enjoy the advantages and opportunities the rest of the nation enjoys. It is basically a condition of inequality.

It is true that many Canadians characterized as poor do not live in conditions as severe as those experienced by many in past generations, nor are as deprived as the many suffering millions in Asia, Africa, and Latin America. But this is small comfort. Around them is a society of riches, of high salaries, and of rising standards...

This condition cannot be measured only in terms of level of income. We have had a difficult time, in the last few years, trying to determine where poverty ends and comfort begins... Most of us never see the members of this separate nation of poverty. They live away from the busy highways and streets we normally travel. They are residents of the isolated pockets of Canadian society and are invisible to most of the community...

The elderly are also caught in the web of poverty. Over half of the over sixty-five age group families, and nearly three-quarters of single individuals over sixty-five have incomes below the minimum level, even while supplying their special needs becomes increasingly expensive... Racial origin can be almost synonymous with poverty in Canada. Our Native population is the most destitute of the poverty-stricken: seventy-five percent of all Aboriginal families make less than $2,000 a year. The average age of death is thirty-three years for the Aboriginal male, and thirty-four years for the female. Inuit suffer the same deprivation.

And, there is the tragic case of the regionally dispossessed. Families caught in areas which have limited assets in our modern rational economy find themselves facing the prospect of tearing up the roots of generations or suffering the continued erosion of hope and livelihood...

Poverty in this country is curable. There is a remedy. I say this not merely as an act of faith, but also as a clear prescription for action. The task of our new century is to learn how to solve difficult problems and how to put our best efforts in service of building a decent, open society. An attack on poverty is the only choice an affluent society has, if it is to honour at all the basic ethic of social responsibly and humanism that is part of our western tradition...

Under the new Department of Consumer and Corporate Affairs we have an opportunity of opening a second front on the federal war on poverty. This new department will have the power to coordinate federal consumer programmes; to provide effective consumer protection in matters of fraud, restrictive trade, and safety; to provide information and research on consumer issues; and in general to develop programmes to enable the consumers of this nation to gain maximum value for the full range of goods and services they purchase and use. This is an important mandate, and one that can be of special use to the many groups of low income, handicapped consumers—the troubled consumers.

For those trapped in the web of poverty, it is crucial to gain maximum use of an income; but the poor are the ones least likely to have the capacity to do so. As study after study shows, it is the poor who pay more for consumer goods of lower quality than the average Canadian housewife does.

It is the low-income consumer who must resort to high-cost credit, with little protection or guidance. It is the resident of our urban or rural ghettoes who does not have access to outlets where comparative shopping and a wide range of goods are possible. It is the uneducated and unsophisticated who are taken in by the unscrupulous seller, who fall prey to unethical advertising, and who too readily get caught in the special kinds of commercial jungles that are spawned on exploitation and fraud...

In a society so oriented towards the consumption of consumer goods, where so much emphasis is placed on the possession of things, and where there is such a high degree of stimulation, the consumer is faced with the bewildering, tantalizing need to grasp the nearest shiny object—a problem of special severity for the family on limited income...

The difficulties of the marketplace are not confined just to those who are stuck in the trap of poverty. There are the young married couples who have very extensive needs but are just at the first level of their earning power. They often over-extend their resources and get caught in a serious spiral of debt. There are immigrants, newly come to Canada, who must rebuild their households in a strange land. Language difficulties and unfamiliarity with the Canadian practises cause confusion in purchasing, and at times can lead them into unhappy situations of being sold useless products at high prices...

Under conditions such as this, there must be programmes designed to secure a better use of the consumer dollar, and better protection for the consumer. Efforts to develop employable skills, create jobs, and increase income will be negated if the increased income leads only to more extensive exploitation of the poor through ignorance, deception, and fraud. The ambitions of the young couple, the new Canadian, and the teenage consumer can be frustrated because of faulty purchases and high debt.

It is for this reason that my own department sees as a first priority the need to mobilize government activity to aid the low-income consumer:

1. One obvious answer is information and education. The effects of having more accurate information about products, of knowing where to buy, how to buy, and what to buy are essential conditions of making better use of income... To begin work in this field, officials in my department have begun planning a pilot project for consumer counselling.

What we have in mind is the recruitment of the services of retired men and women, who have an interest and background in economic or commercial affairs, willing to donate their time to public service. Such individuals may be former businessmen, union co-op officials, or school teachers who would wish to serve in local communities as initiators of this programme of consumer counselling. This person would be available to give advice on matters of credit, real estate dealing, legal protection, buying skills, and financial management. Most important, they would work with existing agencies in areas such as credit unions, settlement houses, fraternal organizations, and church and welfare organizations with a view to establishing consumer programmes of counseling, information, and training particularly relevant to the needs of low-income consumers. In this way, they can act as a catalyst for local community action to repair consumer inequalities...

2. Our plans also include for more stringent and effective enforcement of the laws dealing with matters of fraud, misrepresentation, and restraint of trade. There must be better protection against unethical business practices. We need the cooperation of the provinces to fashion a coordinated and efficient system.

3. Finally, the very presence of a consumer-oriented department in government gives us the opportunity to enact new legislation and influence the development of new policies that can improve the position of the new consumer. The proposed action on drugs is an example. There will be others in the fields of packaging, labeling, weights and measures, misleading advertising, safety, and so on.

These general programmes I outline are, of course, only one part of the overall approach required by the existence of millions of "troubled," low-income consumers—both those caught in poverty, and those who because of age, or youthful inexperience, or lack of consumer skills, find the marketplace restrictive to their ambitions, rather than the asset it should be. No one level of government can provide all the answers, and there must be the concerted and coordinated involvement of the provinces, municipalities, schools, churches, and private groups which have a stake in the consumer's battle. Poverty, like war, is a complex of problems that will not surrender to scattered action. There must be a dedicated, unified response utilizing the best resources and best minds in the country.

So, when we talk about the challenge open to us in this new century, when we think of the greatness that can be ours, we must think in terms of how we build a society open to all citizens, spreading its advantages throughout the population.

The troubled consumer is, of course, only one dimension of the total programme of problem-solving required in the next generation. There is a large inventory of other issues—the state of our cities, the rational development of our resources, the proper use of new communications and new technology, and the direction of our foreign policy. Each of these requires the full mobilization of power and effort in the Canadian community.

The Public Dimension of Advertising
FROM OF A SPEECH TO THE ANNUAL MEETING OF THE INSTITUTE OF CANADIAN ADVERTISING
22 SEPTEMBER 1967 – MONTREAL, QUEBEC

A quarter of a century ago, advertising was a very minor occupation involving a few men and limited expenditure, and it played an insignificant part in the social and economic scheme of things. Today, the business of advertising has mushroomed. The industry employs thousands of talented individuals, spends millions of dollars, and exercises an immense influence on the workings of our modern economy. Last year, Canadians spent two-and-one-half times as much on advertising as on higher education. Much more important, advertising has become a major social institution, responsible for the shaping of tastes, values, and attitudes...

The emergence of advertising as a major social force has provoked searching debate about the role it should play in the community. Foremost among the questions raised is that of what government should do about advertising. On the one hand, critics of advertising have long demanded greater governmental control. They decry what they feel has been excessive commercialization—distortion of the mass media, and the lowering of standards of taste, aesthetics, and health. They claim that advertising creates superfluous needs and wants, and that it encourages wasteful consumption and deliberate obsolescence.

In partial response to these criticisms, government in Canada has prescribed various rules: the Criminal Code and the *Combines Investigation* Act outlaw misleading and fraudulent advertising; the *Trade Marks* Act guards against misrepresentation; there are various regulations on advertising under the *Food and Drug* Act; Agriculture and Trade and Commerce statutes govern the nature of information disclosed and protect against duplicity of falsity...

On the other side of the debate are those who have strenuously defended the advertising business. Some contend that the best role for government is no role at all. They point to the important economic benefits of advertising under a system of free enterprise. They remind us of the danger of invading freedom of expression or restricting the process of communications.

In Canada we have never really made up our mind. There has been only an intermittent and spotty application of the regulations—with little coordinated policy...

This question is of immediate concern to me. The new Department of Consumer and Corporate Affairs, which I head, has the responsibility of directing the federal government's programme for the consumer. It will attempt to ensure that the consumer is fully and clearly informed, that he or she is protected against fraud or misrepresentation, and that standards of safety and health are observed. We want consumers to be informed in a clear and intelligible way about the products they buy, so as to assist them in making the maximum purchase for their dollar.

I also have responsibility for guiding the economic and legal regulatory instruments of government, such as combines, patents, trademarks, corporations, and securities. It will be the concern of the new Department of Consumer and Corporate Affairs that the marketplace is kept competitive, open, and able to serve consumers and businessmen in the most effective manner possible. Our first priority will be to rationalize and coordinate the federal government's own operations. For the advertiser that means that we will seek, in time, to bring some cohesion and conformity to the laws and regulations relating to advertising... Our job will be to improve, strengthen, and tidy up the laws—and to enforce it more uniformly.

We intend to analyze the advertising process and its effect upon the economy and consumer. We intend to pursue the questions of the role of advertising in Canada. Clearly, this new venture of the federal government will have a bearing on the advertising industry.

First of all, it is obvious that advertising is no longer simply a matter of providing snatches of information so that the customer knows where to buy his milk and bread. Advertising is now a highly sophisticated profession. It employs complicated techniques of persuasion and stimulation. It has the power to shape the outlook of Canadians. Advertising can project an image of society that will either be healthy or mediocre; it can instill real choice or create confusion.

The close connection between advertising and the mass media involves a responsibility for the way in which this primary means of communication is used, now and in the future. The revolutionary advances in the technology of communication create vast new opportunities for building a Canadian community of vitality, excitement, and growth—depending on the decisions and choices that are made in its use.

Advertising is also an integral part of the new economy that is now evolving in Canada. The growth of the huge national and multinational corporation, and the commanding position it occupies in the marketplace, have radically changed the classic pattern of economic relationships—of the law of supply and demand...

The power of advertising is undisputed. But power must be balanced by responsibility. How responsible is the advertising man or woman? Has the social and economic power of Canadian advertising been balanced by a sense of responsibility towards the Canadian community?

Let's look at some aspects of the problem:

1. How does the image portrayed in present-day ads relate to a pluralistic community, composed of many kinds of people with many kinds of needs? This is a nation of diversity, and this is part of our strength. But how often is this diversity reflected in our ads?

   The accent is on mass persuasion. The appeal is to one common denominator. Do not our ads show us a society of middle-class images? How often do the faces of minorities appear on national-brand advertising? How much thought is given to the needs of the poor and elderly—emphasizing the quality of goods, or special information that allows them to make effective use of their limited dollar?...

A related question is the role advertising plays in enhancing a sense of the Canadian community. Advertising is greatly affected by the outpouring of American goods. A Canadian identity needs Canadian advertising. Surely we must try to relate our ads to the Canadian context and use the power of communication in the important quest for a Canadian purpose and national unity...

2. What about the problem of choice? We live in the era of the electronic marketplace. The consumer is confronted with a bedlam of competing claims and seductive appeals. Studies show that the consumer is developing a growing resistance to much of advertising's output. Advertising is losing credibility with many people, because it does not uniformly supply them with information satisfactory for the effective purchase of goods. Perhaps the advertiser still underestimates the intelligence, concern, and need of the Canadian consumer and is not keeping in touch with the changing mood of the new consumer...

3. How much attention is given to the needs of public institutions?... I would hope that the Canadian ad industry will seek to match purely commercial persuasion with persuasion on behalf of causes of public importance.

4. What about the economic role of advertising? If analyses are correct, advertising is involving an increasingly bigger percentage of the cost of goods. There is no greater concern today to millions of Canadians than the problem of the rising cost of living. Without doubt, one central key to assessing the role of advertising is the way it influences costs and prices...

5. I know that the advertising industry is now actively discussing the ethics of the trade. There are still far too many cases of ads that mislead or beguile the consumer. Senator Robert Kennedy, in testifying before a US Senate Committee on the Truth-in-Lending Bill, observed that one of the crucial factors in consumer misuse of credit stems from the legal, but distorted, advertising by finance companies...

6. A whole new issue of great significance has been opened by the American courts recently. In the judgment against Proctor and Gamble, the Supreme Court ruled that advertising may encourage

the growth of monopolies. The market power utilized by a larger advertiser can drive small firms out of competition...

7. Advertising must answer for its part in the sharp trend towards blandness, similarity, and triviality in the use of our mass media. Those in the profession of advertising must recognize that they are trustees in a public domain; they are at the switchboard of communications in today's world. As such, their role as powerful agents of social influence implies that standards of purpose and responsibility must be exercised if the advertising industry is to retain the confidence and respect of the public and government.

An Economic Bill of Rights

From a Speech to the Spadina Liberal Association
22 September 1966 – Toronto, Ontario

The whole nature of work and its effect on the economy must be re-examined... where should we start in these reforms?... First, we should examine the right to work and methods of payment. Is there any question that everyone in our society is entitled to work or to be reasonably compensated if work is unavailable... Society must provide work for all who are prepared to work or guarantee a minimum level for those unable to find work...

Second, we should expect the establishment by government of joint labour, management, and government councils, industry by industry. Such councils could... avoid economic and wasteful strife... Three, continuous bargaining between labour and management during the term of collective agreements on technological and other major issues might reduce negotiation by brinkmanship and strikes.

Fourth, worker's security is important. To balance the need for efficiency and modernization in industry, with the need to protect the rights of the workers, funds might be established industry by industry, contributed by management, so that individual workers would not be hurt by change...

Five, labour problems cannot be isolated from the economic inflationary picture. But it is equally important that, when economic guidelines are established, equal emphasis should be given to human guidelines, particularly in times of rising costs...

Six, is not the injunction outmoded? Should our courts be the forum for economic skirmishes between labour and management? Are the courts properly equipped to assess and evaluate the economic and social issues involved in a labour dispute?...

A fresh look at labour and management rights alone is not enough. We should look at all our well-established liberties in a free and open society... In Canada we pride ourselves in our belief that we live in a free and tolerant society. What justification do we have for this pride? The traditional freedoms of speech, religion, and racial equality are recognized... The economic protection of the individual which is equally important should be recognized in our law as well... Changes in our way of life should be reflected in a new Bill of Rights.

But the real need for change lies in the recognition of economic rights. These economic rights should be enshrined in our basic law. We should clearly establish the right to good housing, legal care, and medical care. I believe that Lester B. Pearson will be remembered as a great prime minister in history... (mainly) for his recognition of the new economic rights of man. The Canada Pension Plan, the Canada Assistance Plan, and the Canada Labour Code are all legislative reflections of a great social conscience... But all these massive pieces of legislation will do is readjust the inequalities of the past and the present... it will not cure the problems of tomorrow. It may remedy the inequalities of today, but it does not touch the root causes of inequality. The causes of inequality of opportunity are primarily inferior education and crippling environment. What we must do is to step farther back into man's life and attack these causes of social inequality... This means the removal of barriers and blocks to the door of opportunity for those rewards.

If we are to have a free, rather than a dynastic tradition in Canada, it is important that the economically dispossessed have the opportunity to enjoy the fruits of education... The right to reasonable accommodation at a reasonable price is also a right which should be enshrined in law. It is clear that the environment is the cause of much crime... We have the means and the dollars to provide housing for all of our citizens, but our economic approach to these matters must change...

We must break the crust of indifference to inequality and environment. I sometimes wonder whether our values are right. Price-fixing, slum housing, breach of building by-laws, and income tax evasions are lightly treated compared to some crimes. We have to be tougher about these crimes if we are to achieve in this country a common consensus toward protecting our economic rights. The demand for new economic rights is not a call for a consensus as much as a call to conscience...

From a Speech to the Liberal Leadership Convention

5 April 1968 – Ottawa, Ontario

It has been a long night. We have heard and watched some good men on this platform. All of them with honour, intelligence, capacity. I know them—I admire them all—I would serve under any of them. If anything has been demonstrated tonight it is that this party is the only party ready for the challenge of tomorrow, and deserving of the confidence of all the Canadian people... Some of you have told me that my position on this platform tonight has been a bad break. Number nine, bottom of the batting order. Well let me say this about 9th place—better tonight than tomorrow night... I am not in this race just so you will remember my name at some future date. I am not here now for some "next time." I am not bidding now for your consideration in some vague convention in 1984—perhaps when I've mellowed a bit.

My time is now—and now is no time for mellow men.

I am not mellow. I am restless.

I am restless—for Canada—I am restless to close the gap between the rich and the poor. I am restless to bring our young people into the mainstream of our life. I am restless to reach out and touch, reach out to the disenchanted and the dispossessed.

But I am also restless to see this country start to realize its great potential—in economic matters, certainly (and we can do much more to increase our productivity, our trade, and our real standards of living)—but also to realize the human potential of all Canadians— and of Canada in the world. My concern is with the difficult, puzzling, delicate business of toning up a whole society—of bringing a whole people to that fine edge of morale and conviction and zest that makes for greatness. In any democracy there is always a tug of war between policies to achieve equality and policies to promote excellence. I am certain that Canada can achieve both equality and excellence.

I believe the problems of this country can be solved—if we harness the talents and energy of Canadians everywhere, of everyone here. They will not be solved easily or overnight... Ladies and gentlemen, I represent a choice that is committed to challenge today's problems in a different way. I say our problems can be solved with a new vigour and a new energy that motivates new perspectives, new insights... I want an open society for my country where any Canadian, whether he speaks English or French, whether he was born here or came here yesterday—regardless of where he came from—where any Canadian can go as far in this land—and as high—as his own ability and his own energy can take him. We may not all finish even, but in my kind of country we will all begin even.

Give me your trust and together we can pass the test of today and meet the challenge of tomorrow...

I came to this convention without any commitments—without any encumbrances... Give me your support tomorrow—so that I can give your party back to you.

Our task is to build a party that is strong in all parts of Canada. I was brought up in western Canada and know how the West feels about this party. I have spent considerable time in the Maritimes and know the views of the Maritimes. I have lived and worked for fifteen years in Montreal and have seen, each day before my eyes, the central problem of Canadian unity which has its shapes and forms in Montreal. Hence, I think I have a unique contact with the problems of all parts of Canada—at least I know from personal experience what those problems are.

We must rebuild and strengthen our party organization everywhere. It must not be a party trapped in the big cities... it must be a party that makes sense to the farmers. We want a party where the working man has a say. And it must be a party that welcomes newcomers, especially young people—and anyone who joins us must feel that he or she counts.

We are a group of men and women committed to politics because we believe that a political party is not just a piece of election machinery but a vehicle for reform and for the solution of national problems. We must revitalize the Liberal party. And if we do, no one can beat us in the next election...

This is a restless Canada, a Canada caught in the mood of change... Our mood is restless, not reckless. We must think in terms of reform—but our policies of reform must be realistic, our programs for change must be responsible... Of all the issues, the greatest issue confronting this generation of Canadians is the unity issue... our generation of Canadians must rebuild this country anew. The issue of Confederation will not be solved by confrontation, but by painstaking negotiation... We need practical solutions, not just neat theories... We all have a stake in this... equal opportunity means equal opportunity for all Canadians not just for the "founding races..."

There is one thing I want you to carry out of this hall tonight. Each of us in our heart has tried to define "what is Canada?" But one thing I know—Canada is not an abstraction; Canada is not a theory; it is beyond logic. Our country is not solely a product of the mind, because in many ways it does not make sense. Over the years there are people who have said that it has not been worth the price of being Canadian, and even today there are those who want to break our country up. My answer to them is not in logic, but in the heart. If you cast your vote for me, you will be choosing a Canada that believes in nationalism, has pride in our community, our political sovereignty, our economic integrity.

Chapter 4

The Reformer at Justice

"If liberalism has any criterion," John Turner said, "it is the recognition of the worth and dignity of every individual." When he was sworn in as Minister of Justice in 1968, the dramatic process of law reform which went to the core of defining the kind of society Canadians would have and the rights we would enjoy as individuals was set in motion. Many years later in a dialogue with Turner at Library and Archives Canada, he reflected on the accomplishments of a golden era:

> These were great moments in the history of Canada. We set up an agenda, we brought the country and Parliament along with us and we had a sympathetic prime minister with us every step of the way. Our reforms caused very little fiscal pain; they were years no one could ever take away from us.

The Trudeau–Turner partnership during these historic years was one of Canada's great success stories. The two men often spoke about the challenges and issues of the day informally. They liked and respected one another. Both deeply spiritual and cerebral men, their talents proved complementary. Turner's formidable parliamentary and political skills, his knowledge of the country and his ability to build personal trusting relationships with those of all sides of the floor and in all parts of the country were indispensable to the prime minister. All of these skills were particularly noticeable in the dramatic preparations for the Victoria Conference on Constitutional reform in 1971.

Turner shepherded the massive Omnibus legislation through Parliament—legislation premised on the liberal view that morality was a matter of private conscience and that the criminal law should only reflect the public order. When the national debate over the *Official Languages Act* intensified and its passage was threatened in the House of Commons, the Prime Minister turned to Turner to build alliances in the House of Commons. He enlisted Turner to educate westerners about the legislation in order to head off the anger and apprehension stemming from the misunderstandings regarding the sensitive issue of bilingualism in the public service.

Turner and Trudeau worked closely together during the October Crisis of 1970 throughout the tragic period when Canada lost its innocence and the fragility of our democratic order. Readers are advised to examine the documents of this period on the Library and Archives Canada website, particularly the Cabinet Committee on Security records. The meeting on the FLQ held 15 October 1970, the eve of the invocation of the *War Measures Act*, is particularly interesting. Turner declared at the time that in his view, "the legislation that was now being contemplated was very restrictive and therefore should be justified before Parliament and the country."

As the record shows, the achievements at Justice largely fell into four categories: one, redressing the imbalance in the relationship between the individual and the state (the *Official Languages Act*, the *Expropriation Act*, the *Statutory Instruments Act*); two, the creation of a more contemporary criminal law—credible, enforceable, flexible, and compassionate (the *Omnibus Act*, the *Bail Reform Act*, the Law Reform Commission); three, the promotion of equality of access and equality of treatment before the law for rich and poor alike; and four, bringing the law up to date with technology (the Protection of Privacy bill).

Speculation was rife that the new Justice Minister, who had already acquired a national reputation as a zealous defender of the rights of the little guy, would bring that passion for change to this key portfolio. Evidence of this passion didn't take long to appear, as the graduating students of the Fall Convocation of Osgoode Hall Law School in the Fall of 1968 would learn. The Justice Minister challenged and provoked the graduates, and argued that their role must be to see themselves as agents of social change. Law schools must no longer be conveyer belts graduating students in to the corporate structure he asserted. "If there is justice for some of us, but not social justice for all of us, we dare not speak of the just society for any of us."

In his speech to the North American Judges Association, 1 December 1969, Turner focused on the victimization of the poor. Dramatic action followed. The vast changes in criminal law would ensure it was no longer a crime to be poor. The Bail Reform bill of June 1970, was lauded throughout the country for its humanitarianism. This bill went a long way toward making the law as fair for the poor as it was for the rich. By 1971, Turner had announced initial negotiations with the attorneys-general of the provinces to establish a Canada wide, federally funded legal aid system—a plan he had first unveiled at the Kingston Conference in 1960.

Turner's love of the Canadian wilderness and his will to preserve and protect the environment compelled further reform. As Minister of Justice, he focused on the development of environmental laws which would protect Canada's increasingly threatened clean air, water and land.

Elizabeth McIninch

Frontiers of Law and Lawyership : Legal Education for the Just Society

From a Speech at Osgoode Hall Law School
18 October 1968 – Toronto, Ontario

Today, in an age of confrontation, our social problems become our legal problems. De Tocqueville made that observation years ago. And our problems are legal problems precisely because they are social problems to which the legal process is both relevant and necessary. In a world where the dynamics of social change meet the frontiers of law and lawyership, it is society itself which has become the lawyer's client.

What is the relevance of all this for us as students of the Canadian legal process? Most of us have not even begun to consider that the manner in which the legal profession approaches social problems affects the way these problems are resolved. Some of us have yet to appreciate the fundamental truism that social problems necessarily become legal problems. Yet our legal profession must respond—promptly and creatively—to the fact that society is our client.

For in a rapidly changing complex society, a new social order demands of us new frontiers in law and lawyership. As the state arrogates for itself increasing control over the planning and setting of priorities of all values in society, more and more people are demanding greater and greater protection from the abuses of that administrative process. Conversely, as more and more of these values become possible as personal goals in an increasingly technological affluent society, more and more members of our society are asserting a claim of right to participate in all of these values.

We are witnessing what has been described as "a new search for human values and relationships"—relationships between man and man, and between men and government—that have meaning in the technological and psychological context of our age.

What this search, and the accompanying changes demand is not a law and order that freezes man into predetermined patterns, but a law and order of change, or movement, or options. Yesterday's order, if it is unresponsive, becomes tomorrow's oppression.

Accordingly, just as the shaping and sharing of all democratic values in the just society must not be the exclusive privilege of the few, but the inclusive right of all; so the law must not be the exclusive prerogative of the privileged, but the privileged right of all. All must have equal access to the law. If we are to speak of equality before the law, the law must protect all equally.

If, therefore, the right to bail is the prerogative of the rich, and preventive detention the plight of the poor; if privacy is the right only of those who with counsel claim it, and invasion the deprivation of those who unwittingly suffer it; if society distributes justice only to those who through counsel can claim it, and withholds it from those who without counsel are denied it; if it indulges one class of society but dispossesses another; if, in short, there is justice for some of us, but not equal justice for all of us, we dare not speak of the just society for any of us...

How have we of the legal profession, as architects and guardians of those frontiers of law, responded? Are we responsible for missed opportunities as well as for unfulfilled obligations? We lawyers have been accused of being impervious to change. Some have even accused our profession of being a barrier to change. And what about our law schools?... Students are marched through law school in lockstep in spite of differentiations in interest and their prospective professional careers; while the cadence and rhythm for that lockstep have been set more than a half a century ago, to the orchestration of a radically different social environment...

What about instruction? I have always had the suspicion that our law schools have vacillated between training our students in the technical skills of the art of lawyership and developing a legal mind or enlightened theoretical apparatus. We may have failed in both: in graduating neither the skilled technician nor the critical legal mind. Have we also, in seeking to develop a "legal mind," too often conjured up the static representation of the law as a seamless web of principles existing in a "heaven of legal concepts?" The case method may be positioned on an anachronistic view of the legal process as a technical body of rules existing apart from, rather than as a part of the social process...

Law school curricula nourish the commercial sector. Business law constitutes the core; poverty law and the rights of the dispossessed i.e., the poor, the mentally ill, the illegitimate child and related categories, are relegated to the penumbra, if considered at all. Indeed, it appears at all times as if the curricula of the modern law school have been drawn up by the local chamber of commerce. This is not to suggest that the commercial sector should not be represented on the curriculum; but only that, in an increasingly technological, bureaucratized, and urbanized society, other sectors of society and accordingly of law must be given equal time...

The lawyer must not cast himself as hired gun, or dart thrower, for the privileged class. Law schools must be more than conveyer belts graduating students into the corporate structure. There is, of course, nothing wrong with the lawyer as an advisor to business. There is, of course, nothing wrong with the lawyer function. But the lawyer should also envisage himself as public servant, professional administrator, advocate of special minority interests, and public interest pleader.

What about the second goal of research? Society is the lawyer's client, but how much has the lawyer bothered to learn about society? How familiar have we lawyers become with the behavioural, and biological environmental sciences?—with that scientific knowledge relating to man and his environment? How many of our law professors have the methodological skills to go beyond the mere study of words to investigate the actual operation of the legal process where it counts—in terms of its impact upon the lives of people?

The fact is that we know remarkably little about how the legal process actually operates. We do know that with investment of time and money, we could find out a great deal about it. For instance, we still know very little about what juries actually do. What is the real impact of admitting or excluding evidence which has been illegally obtained? What is the real impact of a particular judicial decision? Who, in fact, receives what kind of penalty, for what kind of offence? How is blame to be divided between a person who commits an act and the persons and environment which laid the groundwork for the act?

What do we really mean when we speak of the "best interests of the child?" The answers to these questions—and hundreds like them—is that we do not know, that we could find out, and that we are still not trying enough to find out...

Finally, how do our law schools qualify in providing an apparatus of community legal services? Do our law students receive the clinical training necessary to equip them as professional men and women involved in the urgent problems of our world? Law is not something in the abstract. A lawyer needs more than a well-furnished legal mind and specialized technical skills. He needs the clinical experience that comes from participation in the urgent, urban issues of our age. Such a clinical program might revolve around a Legal Services agency, or forming substantially the Community Legal Services Agency itself. I am glad Osgoode Hall has made a beginning here.

This need not exhaust the possibilities. Law schools might well explore other available options for clinical involvement. For example, summer or part-time internships with parole boards, the police, administrative agencies and so on. Students should have a wider experience than the legal tome—they should plunge into the turbulence of life itself. They should see and live the law in action.

I believe we must all together ask ourselves these questions about the purpose of a law school—as a forum for instruction, research and clinical community service. Many students are already asking them. Students today are more idealistic about their goals in life and yet they are increasingly skeptical about our society. They don't want to be guns for hire, or dart throwers, for the established interests or values. They want the same law for the privileged as for the dispossessed—for the poor as for the rich. They are trying to define a role for themselves as lawyers in the service of a client that is society itself. We fail both ourselves and them if we offer them anything less.

I am glad our professional Bar associations are re-examining their relationship to the law school and the law student. Our present institutional framework for policing the qualifications of members of the Bar may be both outmoded and irrelevant. Bar examinations, following a content-pattern borrowed from outmoded law curricula, have often little or no relationship to a candidate's competence for the practice of law. What they demand in preparation is the robot memorization of irrelevant minutiae, and the unthinking assimilation of the endless gimmickry and gadgetry peculiar to the local Bar exam—minutiae and gimmickry that will be erased from the candidate's mind within a month of the examination—and at that I may be somewhat generous...

I am aware also that the Law Society is currently reviewing the realities and needs of specialization. We must soon arrive at means of recognizing special legal qualifications or defining standards of competence of the specialist. Nor is there yet any method for determining whether professional competency has been maintained after admission to practice; for our admission system is a one-shot affair, and we have no institutional means for requiring, or even encouraging, members of the profession to expose themselves to continuing education in the law. Here again Ontario has been a leader in this country, but there is much to be done.

Well, I have tried to pose some questions about our law schools and Bar associations—as we examine our legal education in Canada. What now about the Department of Justice? What framework have we been giving for creative expression to the lawyer in his chosen field? Have we, in Ottawa "been doing our thing?" Though the department is the nation's largest law firm, it too often appears to the law graduate as the employer of last resort, rather than the prior and prestigious choice of the best law graduates.

Any department of government is of course only as good, as effective, as the human resources that are available to it. While most law graduates could not be expected to commit themselves initially to a legal career as such in the Public Service, I would like to suggest to you that a two or three year internship or apprenticeship with the Justice ministry would be a rewarding experience for the graduate lawyer. New frontiers, novel ideas, fresh approaches—these are the things that we must seek continuously to renew and that is the challenge that I, as Minister of Justice, and, indeed, the department as a whole, are prepared to accept. Of course, the new, the bright and the different must always be counterbalanced—but we need not be fearful that the countervailing forces of sageness and wisdom, derived as they are from maturity and experience, will always be present. And so, to succeed in building the kind of department that we are striving to build in Ottawa and, indeed, throughout the country, we need your help and your services for at least a limited period—not all of you, of course, but a reasonably representative number of you.

And so I ask you to consider favourably any opportunity to serve that may be opened up to you... Opportunities for specialization will be given, but I hope that no one will suffer from over-specialization, at least during his early, perhaps I should say formative years, as a lawyer. And at the end of the internship, indeed at any stage along the way, a decision can be made to remain with the department, or to use the experience gained elsewhere in the practice of law. I hope many would stay.

Perhaps it would be appropriate for me to mention one or two developments that are receiving consideration at the present time. It is my hope that we will soon be able to establish a National Law Reform Commission to explore on a continuing, rather than on an episodic basis, the frontiers available to our national government to make and amend laws in a just society. The Criminal Law and her areas of federal responsibility would be examined by such a Commission. And it is my thought that such a Commission might well be charged with a particular responsibility involving a continuous evaluation of the fundamental rights and freedoms of the citizens, as these may be found expressed in legislative enactments both old and new.

I also envisage the establishment of a Legal Research Section in the department of Justice where those who have developed a special academic approach and interest in the law may find that they may make a special important contribution in the evolution of our just society. I also visualize that this undertaking may be broadened in the fullness of time to include disciplines other than the law, but rather than risk postulating too much I should perhaps reiterate that these are programmes for the future and it is my belief that they will not be long awaited since they are proper, indeed necessary, ingredients in the evolution of a just society.

We began this afternoon by stating what I believe to be a fundamental truth: that social problems frequently become legal problems. The manner in which the legal profession conceives and approaches those problems will determine the manner in which they are resolved.

And so, the frontiers of the law and of the lawyer must be urgently broadened. Experience has taught us that law and the lawyer are necessary to the reform of our society. In today's rapidly changing world, where a very imperfect law can permeate every inch of our lives, law reform and a constant vigilance for it must be coterminous with the very application of the law itself. Indeed, what is so necessary and so lacking now—and therefore of the greatest challenge and opportunity for the legal profession genuinely concerned with the overall structuring of society. Modern societies, said Raymond Aron, are the first ever to justify themselves by their future, the first in which the motto "man is the future of man" appears not so much blasphemous as banal. If this be so, then the creative frontiers of law and lawyership need not be beyond us; the just society can be a reality in our time. We need no longer ask for whom the bell tolls. It can, and must, toll for all.

Twin Freedoms: The Right to Privacy and the Right to Know

From a speech to the Canadian Bar Association
Annual General Meeting
2 September 1969 – Ottawa, Ontario

In 1890 a young lawyer co-authored an article in the *Harvard Law Review* on the "right to privacy" that was to become a classic of its time. The author defined privacy as "the right of each individual to determine to what extent his thought, sentiments and emotions shall be communicated to others." But the significance of the article resided as much in prophecy as in principle. For in a brief—and sometimes ignored—reference, it warned of "mechanical devices which threatened to make good the prediction 'that what is whispered in the closed shall be proclaimed from the housetops...'"

But if privacy is the most comprehensive of rights, the most comprehensive of techniques is being used to destroy it. While the law lags, technology races; and once again the scientists have beaten the lawyers.

A remote controlled amplifier and microphone no larger than the head of a pin can capture a conversation and transmit it by wire for 25 miles... while wall microphones, of course, can hear and record anything said in such a room... There are transmitters so small that they can be mounted as a tooth in a dental bridge.

The corollary to all this, as revealed in testimony before the House of Commons Committee on Justice and Legal Affairs, is that our telephone can be tapped, our office bugged, our files photographed, our physical movement monitored, our communications recorded—all this without our knowing anything about it or having any right or recourse or any protection in law. The Orwellian society of 1984 may be here already. The open society has become the bugged society. The struggle for freedom is being mortgaged to the parabolic microphone. The zones of solitude are being occupied. There are no more sanctuaries. The erosion of privacy is the beginning of the end of freedom.

How can we over-estimate how important it is to be left alone? Privacy is paramount. Without it a man's friendships become suspect, his trust wanting, his love tainted, his self-respect gone. Imagine a life full of days of being observed by invisible, anonymous eyes, or being listened to by invisible ears. Think of going through life continually looking over your shoulder to try to spot that invisible shadow. The human being in us would suffocate. We would have no real freedom to build a community, to practise our religion or adhere to a political party.

But this is not all. The right to privacy goes not only to the core of our being as individuals, but to the core of our collective being as a society. John Stuart Mill wrote that "the worth of a state in the long run is the worth of the individuals composing it." A state that demeans its citizens demeans itself; a society that mocks the privacy of individuals mocks itself.

In a democratic society, sanctity of communication is essential if its citizens are to have freedom of thought and action. Creativity depends on privacy. Fear or suspicion of surveillance, ever imagined, kills dissent. And when dissent dies, democracy withers. Intellectual controversy is choked. New ideas are stunted. The common weal withers.

During my tenure in Justice, our thrust will be a three-fold one: first, to balance the rights of the citizen against the state; second, to give Canada a more contemporary criminal law—credible, enforceable, flexible, compassionate; third, to promote equality of access and equality of treatment before the law for rich and poor alike.

In a world where the young, the dispossessed, the disenchanted, the urban poor find the state more and more remote; where bigness becomes oppressive, we have to look for ways of restoring the recourses and remedies of the citizen against his government.

The new Expropriation bill, which has been made available to every member of our Association and about which we received scores of helpful comments, represents an effort to strike a blow for the individual against the arbitrariness of state power. We are concerned as well about the difficulty of challenging regulations that may have gone well beyond statutory limits or the scrutiny of Parliament. We shall be broadening the scope of judicial review of decisions of administrative tribunals, and initiating controlling measures over the enabling powers as they appear in the statutes themselves. We are looking forward to new procedures of parliamentary review that will further safeguard the citizen's rights.

Taken then in this context, our efforts to consecrate a legal right of privacy is part of the broad battle of the individual citizen against remoteness and anonymity in government. I start from the proposition that the right to privacy is the most complete of human freedoms and that any encroachment on the right should be allowed only if society has proven that encroachment is necessary.

The department of Justice and the Standing Committee in the House of Commons have been exploring the whole question of the right to privacy with a view to introducing legislation on some aspects of this question during the next session of Parliament...

I should like to address myself to some of the questions we shall have to answer in choosing the various policy options:

1. Should it be a criminal offence to invade privacy by electronic surveillance techniques?

   If there is to be a legal right to privacy and if privacy is to mean anything at all, it must be protected; and if that protection itself is to be meaningful, then all forms of the use of wiretapping or electronic surveillance techniques for the overhearing or recording of private communications must be expressly prohibited and made the subject of criminal offence...

2. If all forms of wiretapping and electronic surveillance are to be made illegal, should there be any exceptions authorizing the use of surveillance devices in specifically limited instances?

   Certainly the law must be reasonable and you need only think of the following items to see the need for some exceptions: hearing aids for the deaf; citizen band radio communications; protection of property by use of closed-circuit TV; necessary servicing of communications systems in order to maintain quality of service...

3. If certain exceptional use of electronic surveillance is to be authorized, who, then, should authorize these exceptions?

   Applications for authorization to conduct electronic surveillance should be made only by the chief of a designated law enforcement authority or his appointed deputy. There is some difference of opinion here as to whether the application should be made to the Attorney General or to the Chief Judge of a Trial Division. As I have stated on other occasions, my personal inclination is that someone who is politically accountable to the people—rather than a judge—should assume the responsibility for that authorization...

4. If there are authorized exceptions, what terms or conditions should be attached to these exceptions for purposes of supervision and control?

   Some of those limiting conditions might include the following:

(a) The grant of any power ought to be "the least possible power adequate to the need proposed." Accordingly, the application for an order should be particular as to the facts and circumstances relied upon by the applicant, the nature of the offence sought to be investigated, the place of interception, the type of communication to be intercepted, perhaps a statement as to whether other investigative techniques have been tried and failed, and the time for which the interception is to be maintained.

(b) No order should authorize the overhearing or recording of communications for a period of time beyond that which is necessary to achieve the order's objective.

(c) Any exceptionally authorized use of electronic surveillance must protect the integrity of privileged communications, unless an additional special need is demonstrated. This would have to be a question of fact to be determined in such a particular case.

(d) All recordings would have to be made in such a way that their authenticity could not be suspect.

(e) Every subject of electronic surveillance must be permitted to have his day in court. The fear of possible unknown surveillance must be lessened. Provision might be made for a civil cause of action whereby an individual would be able to take whatever action might be available to him to recover, where appropriate, civil damages...

(f) Any administration of criminal justice authorizing even the exceptional use of electronic surveillance techniques must contain some provision for a public accounting. Indeed, public support for the exercising of even this limited surveillance can only be obtained where the public can be responsibly informed of the extent and character of its use...

5. If the invasion of privacy is to be made a criminal offence, should evidence obtained illegally without complying with the terms of a new law, be admissible in court?...

By 1980, 80 percent of all Canadians will be housed in less than one percent of our land mass. Our cities will resemble "urban hives." The new cybernetics of an increasingly urbanized technotronic environment will surround us. Science and technology will spawn new forms of electronic surveillance, psychological surveillance and data surveillance. Already scientists are experimenting with brainwave analysis to join the more conventional forms of psychological surveillance such as personality testing and polygraphing... data-generating techniques may well remember what we have chosen to forget. The orbit of privacy will be an ever shrinking one; yet the need for privacy will be more paramount than ever. The law must ensure that the right to privacy remains sacrosanct.

There is another side to the right to privacy which has not received the prominence it deserves, but whose dimensions cannot be ignored. There is a tendency in governments to refuse information to its citizens under the guise of privacy which is disguised as public interest.

Government secrecy is sometimes legitimated as the state's right to privacy, but it may well be a denial of public right to know. If individual privacy is a foundation of democracy, the citizen's right to know is fundamental to any participatory democracy. The public cannot be expected to dialogue meaningfully—still less decide—if it is refused the very information which would make such a dialogue and decision-making possible...

Arbitrary practices, inscrutable executive decisions, can only find acceptance where there is, in fact, no other means or no other way. It must be our constant goal, our continuous endeavour, to circumscribe and eliminate whimsy and caprice in our search for justice.

The right to privacy and the right to know are not contradictory but complementary; they are companion rather than conflicting freedoms. The right to privacy and the right to know are twin freedoms under a democratic order.

The quality of our laws is the measure of the quality of our civilization. Nowhere is this more evident than in the twin freedoms of the right to privacy and the public's right to know. The kind of legislation we succeed in adopting will reflect not only our political ideology, but our political will. A nation's law reflects not only its concern for public order, but its commitment to freedom. The twin freedoms will stand as the measure of that commitment.

I<small>NVOCATION OF</small> J<small>USTICE</small> B<small>ORA</small> L<small>ASKIN AT</small> S<small>UPREME</small> C<small>OURT</small> C<small>EREMONY</small>
28 A<small>PRIL</small> 1970 – O<small>TTAWA</small>, O<small>NTARIO</small>

It is a rare but happy coincidence for a vacancy to exist on the Court at a time when there is a man of the calibre of Justice Bora Laskin to fill it. Indeed, as I have commented elsewhere before, Justice Laskin is that gifted individual who combines in one person the excellence and achievements of many. He is a distinguished legal educator, though his teachings have ranged beyond the contours of law; he is a learned and esteemed Judge whose judgments—and dissents—have become classics in Canadian jurisprudence; he is a renowned labour arbitrator and conciliator, and has investigated labour disputes in such diverse operations as railways, lumbering, communications, hospitals, shipping, construction, movie theatres, and the chemical and electrical industries—and even football; he is a prolific writer of both incisive and imaginative bent; and he is one of Canada's foremost authorities on constitutional law. We are fortunate in Canada to have a man of the stature and excellence of Justice Laskin.

Perhaps the greatest testimony to Justice Bora Laskin was the reception that greeted his appointment. For it was heralded by Bench and Bar alike, by members of academia and scholarship, and by the lay public itself. Justice Laskin has endeared himself not only to the members of his profession but to the members of the community as a whole.

Justice Laskin once said that:
> It is well to keep in mind that the administration of justice has been a social service, a public function with a special blend of private participation... the Judges who are the high priests of the operation have an accountability for their performance... that operates in five directions:
> 1. their accountability to the litigants;
> 2. their accountability to the practising Bar;

3. their accountability to the law schools;
4. their accountability to the legislature;
5. their accountability to the public at large.

Each of these aspects, as Justice Laskin has said, has its special thrust, and in each of these aspects Justice Laskin has been acclaimed. And there can be no greater tribute to a man than the esteem in which he is held by his peers.

Justice For The Poor: The Courts, The Poor and the Administration of Justice
From a Speech to the American Judges Association, San Francisco
1 December 1969 – United States

Few problems are more menacing than the presence of pervasive, life-long, grinding poverty. That we should have poverty in Canada is, as our Economic Council has reported, a disgrace; while the situation in the United States has been brilliantly—albeit painfully—chronicled in Michael Harrington's *The Other America*. The arguments of social academics, then, as to what constitutes the threshold of poverty, or whether there is a cycle of poverty, or whether most of the poor are concentrated in the areas of rural blight, appear not so much brutal as banal. Poverty, simply enough, is pervasive; and poverty, unhappily enough, is present everywhere in American and Canadian society...

The poor know what it means to live lives blighted by poor health, broken families, interrupted schooling, and frequent joblessness. They know what it means to be prey to debt, despair, dependence and crime.

And it is the poor who suffer most from society masked in the trappings of the law. For it is they who are victimized when urban renewal arbitrarily disrupts a neighbourhood; it is the poor who are hurt when creditors garnish wages or repossess furniture; it is the poor who are deprived when welfare agencies deny, reduce or terminate welfare benefits on vague, unarticulated or clearly illegal grounds; it is the poor who are penalized when draconian clauses permit landlords to withhold repairs or capriciously evict them into the street; it is the poor who are hit by bail procedures linked to financial means; it is the poor whose privacy is invaded and whose dignity is denied.

The poor do not use lawyers. They are often thought of as having no need of lawyers. Too many of us think of lawyers as counsellors to corporations, drafters of estate plans or wills, advisors on creditor's rights. But if the poor are rarely plaintiffs they are often defendants; they are bewildered and bemused by legalities they face daily as parents, consumers, tenants, recipients of public assistance and accused offenders. Too often the poor see the law not as a friend but as an enemy, not as an aid but as an adversary, not as a remedy but as an obstacle.

"Laws grind the poor," Oliver Goldsmith said some two hundred years ago, "and rich men rule the law." Two hundred years later poverty is still with us. And the law still does not help the poor. As Justice William J. Brennan of the United States Supreme Court said recently, "Can we honestly protest as untrue the charge that our legal system has built-in bias against the poor, not merely procedural but substantive as well?" Justice Brennan's statement applies with equal force to Canada. Indeed, poverty knows no frontiers. And the law haunts poverty everywhere. Law and poverty provokes a needed inquiry into the nature of our laws and our administration of justice.

Much of what I have to say revolves around private law relationships or legal relations between people. Admittedly, most of these fall within provincial jurisdiction in Canada—or local jurisdiction in the United States. But it is impossible to speak meaningfully about questions of law and poverty without concentrating that discussion on those concerns that touch the poor most directly and most painfully—namely, the day-to-day encounters of tenant with landlord, debtor with creditor, or borrower with lender; and it is precisely these encounters which are increasingly finding their way in the courts, and are beginning to form the subject matter of what may be called "the courts, the poor, and the administration of justice."

This is not to say that questions in the federal public domain—such as the use of the criminal sanction and its impact on the poor, as in the law of bail, or the general burdens of the administrative process which may fall with particular impact on the poor—are not without consequence for the problems of law and poverty; but it is in the contours of daily private relationships among people that the problems of law for the poor present themselves most visibly—or, perhaps one should say, invisibly. As questions of law and poverty, they are matters of national concern; for they reflect and deflect back on the law and the general tenor of the administration of justice in our two countries; and it may well be that, as Judge Skelly Wright has written recently, it is on these issues that the courts, as well as the rest of us involved in the administration of justice, have failed the poor.

For it is here that the actual day-to-day operation of the legal process is most likely to deviate from our hallowed notions about justice for the poor. It is here that we must call into question some conventional assumptions about equality or equal status before the law, equal protection of the laws and equal access to the law. For an analysis of some of our laws reveals the inequality of status, the vulnerability in protection and the inequity in access. The poor are less equal before the law; yet their need is greater.

Let us look first at the question of the quality of status before the law. Justice Brennan's concept of built-in bias against the poor is reflected in the "favoured parties" bias of the law. For the law frequently favours certain parties or roles in a relationship, and the poor are less likely than the rich to be found in these roles. Thus, substantive and procedural law benefits and protects landlords over tenants, creditors over debtors, lenders over borrowers.

The greatest material need of the poor is decent housing. Positive motivation withers in the midst of refuse-strewn alleys, peeling plaster, broken windows, cold radiators and leaky ceilings. The poor inhabit the slums, and the slums dominate the poor. And since the law has generally promoted the interest of the landlord against the tenant in all landlord-tenant relations—regardless of whether the tenant is poor or not—it falls with particular impact on the poor slum tenant...

Finally, public housing laws themselves may also be biased against the tenant. For the contract may be written in such a way as to deny tenants any of the rights commonly associated with tenancy and private housing. In some cases apartments may be inspected at will by management; leases are month-to-month; eviction can occur without recourse to the courts; vandalism on the one hand, and overzealous law enforcement on the other, may be regular appendages; and privacy and dignity may be lacking. In public housing the bureaucratic screen behind which tenants and applicants are dealt with in a disordered and arbitrary manner should be set aside and principles for control of arbitrary action must be applied...

The favoured party bias is perhaps most clearly seen in the creditor-debtor relationship. Indeed, the law here seems to have emphasized the creditor's rights at the expense of the debtor's estate.

Laws which specify the condition under where legally enforceable bargains may be made—and which are the same laws for both creditor and debtor alike—are often, nevertheless, implicitly biased against the poor. Accordingly, while inequality of bargaining power underlies all transactions of buying and borrowing, the poor are especially disadvantaged. They lack the information, training, experience and economic resources to bargain on equal terms with sellers and lenders. Thus, the law which embodies the laissez-faire rule of the market place—"let the buyer beware," and applies to all, whether rich or poor, may be biased against the poor because they find it especially difficult to beware of abuses in the market place...

For while the law may be consistently and evenly applied, it may nevertheless systematically work a hardship on a particular class. And it is the poor who are likely to be victimized by prevailing legal doctrines. For it is the poor who are likely to pay more in the interplay of the market place, though with much less understanding... What is needed here is a greater degree of local counselling and a greater supply of community services. It is in this area that I am happy to say that, in the year and a half that I have been Minister of Justice, I have noticed a developing initiative on the part of Canadian law schools to follow their American counterparts in moving into the neighborhoods and beginning the practice of preventive law...

Finally, the Canadian Department of Consumer and Corporate Affairs is studying the entire bankruptcy law with a view to restructuring the problem of "the debtor's estate" in the hope of rehabilitating the creditor-debtor relationship. As well, certain changes in the *Bills of Exchange Act* are also being considered, although meaningful reforms here would require the cooperation of the provinces.

In questions of favoured party bias, or the problem of equality of status before the law, I suggested that the same law may favour one party at the expense of another. Now I contend that the law may be biased in that the same laws may be applied differently to those who are presumed to be equal. In other words, certain roles are similar or the same for rich and poor—e.g., spouse, father, recipient of government funds, etc. But the laws are applied differently to them in these roles. And so one may find two separate systems of family law—the family law of the rich created, developed and administered by the courts, and the family law of the poor, as public law administered largely through provincial or state or local non-judicial agencies. These agencies are sometimes more concerned with minimizing the cost of relief, than maximizing the rights and interests of recipients.

This dual application of the law applies to the whole question of entitlement under law—and with particular reference to entitlement to government largesse. In other words, the government has one set of rules for dispensing benefits to the poor in questions of public assistance and welfare law, and another for dispensing largesse to the rich in questions of licenses, subsidies to the economy and government contracts...

We have traditionally regarded courts as the site of adjudication. But issues of adjudication involving the poor frequently arise in administrative settings where cases are commonly processed without the benefit of an adversary system or conventional procedural safeguards. Moreover, the lower the level of judicial system, the more likely it will be dealing with the poor, the greater the increase in caseload, and the greater tendency towards mass processing of cases. The poor get less attention, less time and less skill...

The criminal law sanction is the paradigm case of the controlled use of power in society; and it is the courts—particularly the lower courts—to whom the administration of criminal justice and the arbitration of this uniquely hazardous sanction is entrusted.

Indeed, it is in these lower courts that the quality of criminal justice must be measured, for as many as 90 percent of the criminal cases in this country are settled at this level. Though the Supreme Court and Appeal Courts set precedents and receive wide publicity, it is the municipal courts that comprise the judicial system of most relevance for the vast majority of accused persons. And so it is probably of no small concern for judges like yourselves to find the Report of the President's Commission of Law Enforcement and the Administration of Justice concluding as follows:

> Every day in the courthouses of metropolitan areas the inadequacies of the lower courts may be observed. There is little in the process which is likely to instill respect for the system of criminal justice in defendants, witnesses or observers.

> This finding has been corroborated by the report of your National Commission on the Causes and Prevention of Violence, which declared that the courts are "more turnstiles than tribunals." It has been argued that some courts have even become an arm of the law enforcement process...

Some of you may regard this analysis as extravagant or even irrelevant to the American scene... if we are to have any appreciation of the impact of the criminal law sanction and the administration of criminal justice on the poor, we must begin by disabusing ourselves of some time-worn mythology, mythology that has served as a self-protective mechanism:

(i) We must disabuse ourselves of the myth that the criminal law process can be understood within the contours of the adversary system. The criminal law process can really only be understood by threading its impact from the initial phase of the "low visibility" discretionary decisions to invoke the criminal law process in the first place, to the final disposition at the time of sentencing.

(ii) We must disabuse ourselves of the myth that there is, indeed, an adversary system of criminal justice at all; for the criminal justice system is more administrative than adversarial; and at times more non-system than system.

(iii) We must disabuse ourselves of the myth that the criminal law sanction falls with equal impact on all segments of society. Indeed, it may well be—as some studies have pointed out—that our laws, such as vagrancy and public drunkenness—and our courts that administer them—have made it virtually a crime to be poor in public. And so it is that the condition of poverty may become the rationale for criminalization.

(iv) We must begin to question our self-appointed role as "moral entrepreneurs" of criminality, particularly where the decision to criminalize may be one of aesthetics—i.e., "the unattractive public poor"—rather than actual criminality.

(v) Finally, it may well be that our decision-making about the orbit and impact of the criminal sanction on people is predicated on certain assumptions about man and the social order which may not be demonstrable empirically or even valid scientifically.

And yet, through it all we persist in making these judgments and perpetuating these myths.

Justice in a society such as ours, a society marked by wide differences in wealth and power, requires a legal system that compensates for these differences. The law is, above all, a means of creating and protecting rights. What is so necessary is an enlarged conception of the rights of the poor and a changing conception of the role of law in providing, protecting and implementing these rights. We must disabuse ourselves of the myth that poverty is somehow caused by the poor. We must recognize that the law often contributes to poverty. We must understand that the law appears always to be taking something away. That we have to change. And those of us who have been given the temporary custody of our laws by the people must ensure that those laws and our courts treat all equally—rich and poor alike.

The Law and Pollution

From a Speech to the Annual Meeting of the Galt Chamber of Commerce

28 January, 1970 – Galt, Ontario

Eight years ago, Rachel Carson wrote *The Silent Spring*. In the opening chapter, called a Fable for Tomorrow, Miss Carson speaks lyrically of a place that could very well be Galt, or any other similar cities and towns in this region. The author writes as follows:

> There was once a town where all life seemed to live in harmony with its surroundings. The town lay in a checkerboard of prosperous farms... where in spring, white clouds of bloom drifted above the green fields... Even in winter, the roadsides were places of beauty where countless birds came to feed... Then a strange blight came over the area and everything began to change... mysterious maladies swept the flocks of chickens... The farmers spoke of much illness among their families.

Today, the "fable of tomorrow" has become the reality of today... Indeed, the fifth horseman of the Apocalypse—pollution—is riding towards us. Water is our greatest national resource; yet one hundred yards from the House of Commons the Ottawa River—one of the largest in the world—is dying" Unspoiled land ought to abound in Canada but it is becoming an increasingly rare resource and land, unlike air or water has no antibodies to dilute pollutants... So it is, then, that there are few among us who have not been exposed to the noxious doses of chemicals, wastes, fumes, noise, sewage, and heat...

To some scientists, the fifth horseman of the Apocalypse may arrive sooner than we think—and global disaster may result if environmental pollution continues unabated... Our planet is already well advanced toward a phenomenon called "the greenhouse effect." But as Mark Twain used to complain, everyone talked about the weather, but nobody did anything about it, and so it is with pollution. Rhetoric is a blind alley. Indeed we could do without a smog of words. For if the war on pollution is to be won—if indeed it is to be fought at all—a comprehensive national and international legal regime will have to be developed and applied. For what is needed is a hybrid prevention-control model, and law is nothing if not a prevention-control strategy... The environment cannot only be the concern of ecologists; it must be the concern of lawyers and legislators and ordinary citizens everywhere.

Such a legal regime would necessarily be organized around such variables whose legal base forms the core of any prevention-control model... It would reflect the following imperatives: first, we must create new regulatory institutions with alternative regulatory controls, (i.e. penal, taxing, injunctive, etc.), corresponding to the variables in pollutants and polluters to be regulated;... second, we must deal with vested economic and community interests and the pressures they generate.

We must make sure that our depollution policies are not impeded by special interests indifferent to the public interest; three, we may have to analyze the notion of the right of the person to use his own property as he sees fit;... four, we must translate our strategy for the war on pollution into recognition of individual and collective rights of ordinary citizens to a clean environment...

For do we not have the right to clean air? Do we not have a right to enjoy clean and fresh waters? Do we not have a right to be free from damaging noise?... Citizens, then, may want to explore their legal rights against polluters. Governments should consider legislation permitting the state to "recover" from polluters; and five, we must cooperate in developing an international regime to deal with pollution on a global scale...

In general, present international arrangements have powers of an investigatory and recommending nature, but no sanctioning or enforcing provisions. This seems to be a general limitation of all international legal regimes to control pollution. As well, we are going to have to move into the North to establish pollution control zones to protect our coastal seas and arctic regions...

If the war on pollution is to be won, we will all have to radically refashion our ideas about the relationship between man and nature. For if we are to have any effect at all, we must abandon our "vandal ideology" which has permitted us to ravage our environment... Give earth a chance. If we do so, we may find that our environment will give us a chance as well.

Reflections on the War Measures Act
FROM A SPEECH TO THE YALE POLITICAL UNION
16 APRIL 1971 – UNITED STATES

There is an old Chinese curse which says—and not without a good deal of irony—"Blessed are those who live in interesting times." For a long time now Canadians seem to have escaped this curse. There are those who seem to have escaped this curse. There were those—and there are still—who regard our lives as uninteresting, our politics as irrelevant, our existence as banal. Indeed, your own *Newsweek Magazine*, in a cover story on Canada during our October crisis, seemed to imply that Canada had a patent on "uninteresting times;" we have developed, it has been said, a monopoly on banality. In a sense, however, it is a perversion of the times that the very banality of violence judges a non-violent existence as banal! But while others mocked our innocence, we smugly assumed it—and were even comforted by it.

Since October, 1970, all that has changed. Canadians have experienced what Toffler would have called 'future shock.' And so it is Canadians who smiled complacently when Mao's Red Guards raged in the streets, or looked on condescendingly when troops used tear gas at Berkley, or the National Guard fixed bayonets in Chicago, (but then) woke up to find the Canadian army patrolling the streets and a piece of legislation—the *War Measures Act*—intended for proclamation in a time of war being invoked in a time of peace.

What then is this legal animal? Under what authority was the government acting? What reasons were given by the government to justify this proclamation? What controls, if any, existed? What impact was there on civil liberties and the Canadian *Bill of Rights*? What impact might it have on the future of Canadian society in general, and the constitutional and political process in particular?

These are some of the questions I would like to discuss with you this evening, and relate to comparative counterpart approaches in the US, wherever appropriate and where useful for purposes of our discussion. But before answering these questions, or in order to approach them from the perspective of Americans, let me try and encapsulate for you some of the fundamental principles of the Canadian constitutional process and how it differs from the US.

The organizing principle of the Canadian constitutional process is the federative principle; and Canada embodies the notion stated by your own eminent jurist, Roscoe Pound, who said, "A federal polity necessarily becomes a legal policy." It is this "legal federalism" which characterizes the Canadian political process. It is predicated on the thesis that the total grant of legislative powers—the totality of self government—is contained in the legislative powers possessed by the federal and provincial governments. The main constitutional concern, then, is which government is legislatively competent to do what?

Accordingly, an alleged denial of civil liberties would be approached by asking the following question: Is the alleged denial of civil liberties within the competence of the denying government? If it is, that would be the end of the matter, notwithstanding that it may involve a deprivation of civil liberties. Accordingly, in cases where such deprivations have appeared to be particularly offensive to the judiciary, it might rationalize its decision not by saying that what a government did was unconstitutional in the sense that it denied civil liberties, but that it was unconstitutional in the sense that it was beyond the legislative competence of that government to do what it did. But it leaves the unhealthy feeling that if presumably the denying government had had the legislative competence to do what it did, then those civil liberties could have been denied. The concept, therefore, of "unconstitutional" is usually approached in the sense *ultra vires*, i.e., whether it is beyond the legislative competence of the denying government rather than in terms of unconstitutional in the sense of contrary to fundamental law and fundamental rights.

A second and derivative principle from this legal federalism is that of the sovereignty of Parliament. Parliament, then, is the pre-emptive decision-making organ involving, therefore, somewhat of a deviation from the principle of separation of powers and checks and balances as reflected in your constitutional process.

The role of the judiciary, then, as a corollary to the principle of the sovereignty of Parliament, has been characterized by judicial restraint rather than judicial activism. The court has, time and time again stated that it will not substitute its judgement for that of the legislative and that it will not make law; and that if there is to be a redress of grievance or a restoration of civil liberties, that will have to be done by the legislature. This judicial deference has sustained the viability of the doctrine of *stare decisis* in Canadian jurisprudence, and, as I said earlier, if a denial of rights is particularly offensive, judicial ingenuity has found a means of both rationalizing it in terms of *stare decisis* and protecting the rights involved not on the grounds that these rights were to be protected intrinsically, but on grounds that they were beyond the legislative competence of the denying government...

Finally, in 1960, the federal government passed a Canadian *Bill of Rights* designed to make civil liberties a separate legislative issue rather than one to be subsumed only within the question of legislative competence of the denying government. But even this bill has its limitations. It is not entrenched in fundamental law as is your *Bill of Rights*. It is a statute of Parliament and therefore subject to repeal, amendment, etc. by any successive act of Parliament. It applies only to federal legislation and has no application whatsoever to provincial laws. It seems to freeze certain rights as of a given moment in time without any rights expansion potential. And finally, notwithstanding a celebrated application of the Canadian *Bill of Rights* last year in *Regina vs Drybones* wherein the Supreme Court of Canada declared inoperative a provision of the *Liquor Act* which discriminated against Indians (sic) in the Northwest Territories, the judiciary has been restrained in its interpretation and application of the Canadian *Bill of Rights*.

The cumulative impact of these organizing principles of Canadian constitutional law has been a rather undeveloped sensitivity—certainly in comparison with the United States—to civil liberties... Paradoxically, the whole exercise with the *War Measures Act* in October 1970 may have the long-term effect of sensitizing Canadians to their civil liberties in ordinary times, rather than a concern for them only in a time of civil emergency.

1) Some intellectual caveats for purposes of discussion.

I think it is useful, however, for purposes of a critical and meaningful exchange, to bear in mind two intellectual caveats in approaching the issue of Canada's *'Crise d'octobre'*—the October crisis. First, the government and it's supporters in respect of the invocation of the *War Measures Act*, are not the only pro-Canada people, nor are those who objected—and object—to the government's decision somehow unpatriotic or less "Canadian." Secondly, and conversely, one should not automatically regard the government and it's supporters as somehow being anti-civil libertarian or that the only true civil libertarians are those who opposed the government's decision. There are, then, good Canadians and good civil libertarians on both sides of the issue, and one should, therefore, approach it in "issue-oriented" terms. One should ascribe legitimacy to a position in terms of its intrinsic legitimacy *qua* issue rather than in terms of whether one takes a pro or anti approach to the issue. Legitimacy should be a function of advocacy rather than labelling.

2) Nature and Sources of legal authority for the Proclamation of the *War Measures Act*

a) The *War Measures Act* is a statute of Parliament first enacted in 1914. It is a classic example of enabling legislation which, in this case, authorizes the Governor in Council—or Canadian Cabinet—to proclaim it whenever "…by reason of the existence of real or apprehended war, invasion, or insurrection, it is deemed necessary or advisable for the security, defence, peace, order and welfare of Canada." The source of legal authority, then, is Parliament speaking through the *War Measures Act*; the Canadian Cabinet acts only in virtue of a right of exercise delegated to it by Parliament—and through Parliament, the people themselves.

b) The *War Measures Act* is a clearly and extraordinary, if not drastic, remedy. It is the only enabling legislation of its kind available to the government, and it can only be proclaimed by the Canadian Cabinet. No province—and no Premier of any province—and no body other than the Canadian Cabinet can proclaim the *War Measures Act* and thereby proclaim a state of "martial law." Unlike the US, where, I understand, there exists a number of statutes enabling the exercise of emergency powers, and unlike those statutes enabling even Governors of states to exercise these powers, the Canadian recourse is unambiguously—if drastically—clear.

c) The *War Measures Act* is the most open-ended enabling legislation on the statute books. It essentially authorizes the government to do almost anything at all. For example, the government could make any regulations whatsoever, including deportation, censorship, limitations on freedom of movement, etc. But it is important to note here that the only authority which the Canadian government has in legal terms is that authority which grants to itself through regulations made pursuant to the proclamation of the *War Measures Act*. In other words, the sanctioning impact of the *War Measures Act* is restricted to such regulations as authorized by the Canadian Cabinet. These are the only "zones of operation." This is the only "law" and so the proclamation of the *War Measures Act* in October 1970, must be seen in terms of the regulations made pursuant to it, rather than in terms of the potential grant of legislative authority inherent in the act at the time.

d) The legal and operational impact of the *War Measures Act*, then, should be seen in light of the Public Order Regulations, the main characteristics of which are as follows:

i) the FLQ, and any other organization advocating the commission of crimes or the use of force as a means of, or as an aid in accomplishing governmental change in Canada, was declared to be an unlawful association; and any person who was a member of, or who committed any of a number of acts relating to that illegal association, such as advocating or promoting its aims, communicating statements on behalf of, contributing dues for the benefit of, etc., was guilty of an indictable offence and liable to imprisonment for a term not exceeding five years.

ii) Special police powers regarding arrest, detention, and search and seizure, were also authorized to facilitate the investigation, detection, apprehension and detention of those suspected of having engaged in criminal activities...

e) Finally, in terms of the nature and authority regarding the *War Measures Act*, it should be noted that the Canadian Cabinet is not required to disclose the reasons upon which it acted in invoking the *War Measures Act*. Section two of the Act states that the issue of proclamation "shall be conclusive evidence that... an insurrection, real or apprehended, exists." The declaration, then, is self justifying and is a classic example of an absolute privacy clause, i.e., all other organs of government—and for present purposes, one might speak in terms of the judiciary—are excluded from questioning the legitimacy of invoking that proclamation...

3) Controls over the exercise of the *War Measures Act* and the Public Order Regulations

All this should not suggest that there are no controls available in respect of a capricious, arbitrary and illegal governmental invocation and application of the *War Measures Act*. For the government is obliged to lay the proclamation forthwith before Parliament and any ten members can ask that it be debated, and through debate, repeal it...

Within two weeks of proclaiming the *War Measures Act*, our government introduced legislation which has since been passed by Parliament in the form of the *Public Order Act*, and which replaces the Public Order Regulations authorized by the *War Measures Act*. This *Public Order Act*, which is due to expire on the 30th of this month, is much more circumscribed both in terms of the definition of what constitutes an illegal association, as well as in terms of the special police powers of arrest, detention, and search, and seizure.

One should not ignore the controls generated by informal institutions of decision-making, i.e., the media, protest groups, civil liberty associations etc...

REASONS FOR INVOKING THE *WAR MEASURES ACT*

As I mentioned earlier, the government is not obliged to disclose the reasons upon which it acted. Nevertheless, in statements by various members of the government, and the prime minister in particular, these reasons became evident. First, the federal government received requests from both the Province of Quebec and the Municipality of Montreal declaring that an apprehended insurrection existed and asking the federal government to invoke the *War Measures Act*. Second, there had been the kidnappings of a British diplomat, James Cross, as well as a Quebec Cabinet Minister, Pierre Laporte, together with threats of further kidnappings and possible assassinations. Third, there were 2,000 pounds of dynamite running loose in Quebec and the threat of possible synchronized remote controlled bombings of power installations, public service centers, etc.

Finally, there was—together with the escalating exhortations to violence, and, an increasing fear and acute anxiety in the Quebec population—an erosion of public will and a breakdown of civil order. What was resulting, therefore, was a "critical mass" of apprehendable insurrection. The options then available to the government at that point were either the joints of our criminal law, as Kleindienst has put it, or the extraordinary and drastic option of the *War Measures Act*.

Unfortunately, the criminal sanction was perceived as being inadequate to cope with the apprehended insurrection... For the existing criminal law was not designed to deal with organized terrorist movements, which, by the use of synchronized violence, can hold a technocratic society up for ransom. Accordingly, it follows that no matter how criminal in nature an organization might be, membership in itself would not be unlawful. And when the conclusion is reached that society must defend itself against the very existence of an organization like the FLQ, then that organization must be outlawed. The aim of outlawing the organization, then, is to render it ineffective by placing its membership in jeopardy, eliminating sources of support, crippling its ability to communicate, and so on. There comes a point when a government cannot tolerate the operation of an illegal parallel power threatening the fabric of government and the lives of its citizens.

The impact of the *War Measures Act* and the *Public Order (Temporary Measures) Act* on Canadian society in general and the constitutional process in Canada in particular was:

a) In the short run, and speaking in strategic terms, the whole exercise succeeded in dismembering the FLQ, severing it from its logistical supports, restoring the general will, and renewing the vitality of a citizenry that had undergone deep anxiety and anguish.

b) The long run impact raises on the one hand some important questions of a constitutional nature and important concerns of a societal nature... Does the invocation of the *War Measures Act* unnecessarily disturb the equilibrium between the Executive, the Parliament, and the Judiciary? How do we control the possibilities for the abuse of executive discretion? What do we mean when we speak of an apprehended insurrection?... Should a minimum threshold requirement be that of a clear and present danger or its functional equivalent?... Should the judiciary be entitled to enquire into whether a state of apprehended insurrection existed?... What is to happen to our Canadian *Bill of Rights* in the invocation of the *War Measures Act*?... How adequate is our Criminal Code to deal with civil emergencies?...

But there are serious questions as well in respect to the future of Canadian federalism. Will our experience unify us or polarize us? Will we become more sensitive to Quebec in Canada and the French Canadian community or will this desensitize people to the needs of the political social contract? Will we become more vigorous in our practice of civil liberties in ordinary times or will we just be concerned about abuses in emergency situations? What, then, will be the aftershock of the October crisis?

It has not been easy for the Canadian people, programmed for and proclaiming non-violence, secure and secured in the belief that it "can't happen here," and yet to sense somehow that it has. Canada, it has been said, has lost its innocence—and it may well be true... But if Canadians were philosophically and psychologically complacent, our law was no less so. It is often said that a people's law is a measure of a people's civilization, and while this may hold forth great promise for a reform oriented people in a time of peace, it may leave that people vulnerable in a time of insurrection.

Our ordinary criminal law, then, did not anticipate and was both operatively and philosophically unprepared to cope with a state of apprehended insurrection in peacetime; and the *War Measures Act*, intended to cope with a state of apprehended insurrection in war, was unprepared for invocation in a time of peace. But faced with these two alternatives, there was no alternative. The temporary abuses of civil liberties—however offensive and abhorrent that was to our philosophy and to our sensibilities—had to be preferred to the risk of the apprehended insurrection occurring and the social convulsions thereby unleashed.

It was not an easy choice—in a way, a very tragic one. But no government entrusted with the security of its people and the protection of their liberties could have done otherwise. If it did, it would be acting treasonably to its own people... For the rule of law is the essential condition not only of the existence of the state but of the existence of individual liberty within the state. Freedom is the pre-condition of liberty, and restraint is the beginning of freedom. The rule of law is the source and condition of that restraint, and through it, therefore, of freedom and liberty for the individual and the collectivity. Violence, therefore, is not only a denial of the democratically constituted authority of the state or its members existing as a community, but a denial of the liberty of the individual himself...

The causes of violence run deep. The sources of alienation that provoke such violence run deeper still. What we did was to meet violence in the short run; but this must not deter us from what needs to be done in the long run to rip out the social and economic abuses that breed the frustration and anger that brings out the worst violent streaks in men and women. And so it is that we have turned our attention to the road of law reform and the continuing enhancement and protection of civil liberties...

We have become very aware of the fragility of a democratic order. The very strengths of democracy are also its weaknesses. The very liberties we strive to enshrine can become by excess the licence that can destroy. There is no freedom without order under the law, and there can be no order under the law without freedom.

May 11, 1963   St. Ignatius Church, Winnipeg, JNT and GMT

94 POLITICS OF PURPOSE

August 1970 Lake of the Woods, JNT, Elizabeth, Michael, and GMT

August 1981   Coppermine River, NWT, David, Andrew, Elizabeth, JNT, GMT, and Michael

August 1981 Muskox Rapids, Coppermine River. Turner family canoeing a part of the Coppermine River, GMT, David, JNT, Michael (back), Elizabeth, and Andrew

August 1989 Lake of the Woods, JNT, Michael, and David

August 2000   Lake of the Woods, David, Michael, Elizabeth, Andrew, GMT with Toby, and JNT

September 1985   JNT at the helm while sailing around the Queen Charlotte Islands with Bill Reid and others.

June 4, 2004   JNT at a World Wildlife Fund meeting in Lunenberg, NS

The House of Commons Heritage Collection
The Right Honourable John Napier Turner, Prime Minister, 1984
© *House of Commons Collection, Ottawa*

Chapter 5

The Canadian Identity

One of John Turner's mentors as an adolescent was the late A.L. Cochrane, who taught him how to canoe and survive in the wilderness at a summer camp north of Ottawa. In a moving, very perceptive biography entitled *The Long Run,* Jack Cahill wrote:

> And despite his many track and field successes, these are the recreations he loved best... his usually clipped and pragmatic phrases become poetic as he talks, even today of the Canadian wilderness, as if he believes there must be a mystic bond between a true Canadian and the land itself; that he must be able to respect and challenge its rivers and mountains and lonely wildlands in order to be a real part of it and to understand it.

The friendship between Cochrane and Turner, developed at a young age, grew when Turner became part of the Arthur Laing team at Northern Affairs and Natural Resources, 1963–65. By plane, snowmobile, truck and canoe, Turner did inspection tours with Cochrane. This was an exciting and adventurous period in which Turner and his colleagues thought through the challenges of conceptualizing, then constructing the infrastructure needed to govern this immense territory, comprising 40 percent of Canada's landmass.

Turner's love of the north is evident in his speaking notes over the decades. In an extemporaneous, very emotional speech given at Pond Inlet when the then Justice Minister was admitted to the Bar of the Northwest Territories, he thanked Justice Morrow "a judge at the top of the world."

> looking out through the schoolhouse, and probably on as magnificent scenery as any man or woman could see anywhere, bright, white clad, a land of glacial wonder, mountains and fjords; you are the judge who must take the longest circuit and the longest trip in the world, bringing justice to the people.

As Justice Minister, Turner would initiate the legal aid review of July 1969 in the Northwest Territories. He undertook this upon the recommendation of Mr. Justice Morrow—nine years after the presentation of his celebrated paper on legal aid at the historic Kingston Conference.

Turner's deep understanding of the Western mosaic made him indispensable to Prime Minister Trudeau in the latter's attempts to head off public misunderstandings over the potential implications of the *Official Languages Act*. That instinctive, easy-going relationship with westerners is particularly evident in "A Nation's Commitment" a speech he gave to Edmontonians in 1969.

When Canadians listened to the great trade debate on the evening of 25 October 1988, they heard Turner say, as he had many times before, that "this is more than a debate about trade." It was a debate about "the kind of Canada we intend to leave to our children." It was about the soul of the Canadian identity he loved and in which he so fervently believed. In his speech on becoming Liberal leader and prime minister designate, given 16 June 1984 in Ottawa, he quoted Arthur Lower who wrote long ago:

> in every generation Canadians have had to rework the miracle of their political existence. Canada has been created because there has existed in the hearts of its people a determination to build for themselves an enduring home. Canada is a supreme act of faith.

From that act of faith, Canadians built the most free, most tolerant country in the world. We conclude this section with Turner's speech to the Liberal leadership convention in Calgary June 1990.

Elizabeth McIninch

A Second Canada—the Reach for Resources
From a Speech to the B.C. Weekly Newspaper Association
28 October 1966 – British Columbia

The surest path to economic freedom is the creation of new sources of wealth. Here lies the key to Canada's future. The speed with which we develop our national resources will determine the tempo and pace of our economic independence. But first we must satisfy ourselves as Canadians that we have made a deliberate decision to harvest our resource... We have not yet devised a resource strategy which can be translated into terms that can be understood by all Canadians. For instance, have we done all we can to open up our north? Why shouldn't we have a system of labour incentives to attract skilled workers to the north? Why not a system of tax incentives for capital development in the north? Why shouldn't we have a policy for the equalization of living costs as between our north and our south?...

Research is the essential first step. Today we have techniques for the gathering of information which were undreamed of but a few years ago. We must harness these new techniques in a sophisticated and effective way. We need research in soil conditions and climate. We need a thorough inventory of our renewable and non-renewable resources. We must complete our aerial surveys and our aero-magnetic surveys of the north...

Emigration from our south to our north is essential to any development of our resources, and yet very little research or thinking has gone into our policies in this area. We have done little to attract new citizens to our north. Instead, we have concentrated almost all our attention to life and growth within a hundred miles of the forty-ninth parallel... The north has always been a great teacher. Give us men and women from the various nations of the world willing to work and to learn, and with a lust for success... We must think very soon of making the cost of living and the price of doing business in the north more equal to those in southern Canada. We need, in other words, a northern equalization policy...

A national resource policy for Canada is imperative. Resources know no boundaries. We need national principles and concepts to guide us in the development of our national resources—a national policy. Not a unitary policy, but a unified coordinated one... The development of our resources—particularly those in our north—could raise the standard of living for all Canadians. This is a call to open up Canada for the future... We must compete now for young Canada's allegiance to this country by throwing out a challenge... We will require all our skills of leadership to focus public attention on the priorities of our north and the benefits of resource development...

In my days as Parliamentary Secretary to Arthur Laing, now the Minister of Indian Affairs and Northern Development, I came to love it and to realize its potential. I could have had no better apprenticeship. I only wish that all Canadians could have a similar opportunity to see the north, to sense the secret it holds for Canada's future. The second Canada—the Canada of tomorrow—must have a vibrant north, pouring out its riches to all of Canada, forging into the cold reaches of that country, a steel-hard economy, sharp enough to cut away pockets of poverty, strong enough to meet our bold aspirations, bright enough to fire our imagination and our hopes.

With dynamic government and with high-spirited men and women throughout the country we can meet and fulfill the aspirations of the second Canada. Bruce Hutchison, in his book *The Unknown Country*, brooded about our future. He said:

> My country has not found itself, nor felt its power, nor learned its true place. It is all visions and doubts and dreams ... We have not yet grasped ... the full substance of it in our hands, nor grasped its size and shape. We have not yet felt the full pulse of its heart, the flex of its muscles, the pattern of its mind ... But now our time has come and we are ready.

Yes, I believe we are ready.

Every Canadian has an acute and inner sense that the membranes of this country are stretched thin over a land that may be so disparate in composition, so tense in its inner relationships, so enmeshed in its silent fears and antagonisms, and so entrapped by history, that it cannot fulfill its destiny. There is no place for that kind of collective pessimism. History does not linger long in one place. Canada has a choice. We can become a mere footnote to history, because we failed to live up to our rich potential, or we can become a glorious page in the annals of man. This is your challenge and mine. To this task we must all be dedicated.

A Nation's Commitment

Excerpts from a Speech given to the Canadian Club
8 April 1969 – Edmonton, Alberta

Let me begin by saying that I understand the psychological gap between east and west: the feeling of remoteness from decision-making centers; the feeling that western priorities are being disregarded by eastern power brokers. Perhaps, instead of talking about unity and language, you think I should bear down on some problems of immediate importance to Alberta and Western Canada: such as resource development; taxation policy; economic growth, the cost of living and inflation; wheat and the National Oil Policy; the future of the Canadian North (Edmonton is the gateway); housing, trade and the Pacific rim. These are the "gut issues" for western Canada and we in Ottawa are concerned.

Personally, and by my own up-bringing as a westerner, I am very concerned. Western MPs are becoming more vocal, insistent, even rebellious—there is a large western contingent on the government side which is carrying a lot of weight and forcing the western view on the cabinet. I am deeply sensitive to the western outlook—but I have an obligation as Attorney General to speak to certain national problems that relate to my current responsibilities. These are, of course, federal–provincial relations. Language is part of these responsibilities.

People in this part of the country may feel remote from Quebec; we, with federal responsibilities, have a duty to try to preserve Canada in its present geographical and territorial form. We have to keep Quebec in Confederation by all reasonable measures and at any reasonable price...

The basic question is whether the French language will exist in Canada or outside of it—in a separate Quebec. This is the basis of the current constitutional debate. This is the basis of the Official Languages Bill.

I know it is difficult for the people of western Canada to digest. Here, we find a mosaic of many cultures; a melting pot where there has been overall an assimilation into the English language. To you, the Official Languages Bill appears to be a reversal of history... But the fundamental premise behind it? This country, as we know it, can survive only if we broaden our recognition of two founding cultures and two official languages.

I want to say a few words about the bill and its importance for the future of the country. I believe that the provisions of the bill have been generally misunderstood, especially in the western provinces. Some people seem to feel that the bill will oblige—will force—the average citizen to speak another language—that it represents compulsory bilingualism. This is not so. The principle is equality of access, so that every citizen can communicate with his or her federal government in either language; it is not compulsory bilingualism for people. People will continue to use their own language. That's the point...

Why two languages? This is a political fact and the territorial and geographical unity of the country demands it. Quebec is 80 percent French Canadian. For the young generation, the options are Canada or Quebec. The option for Canada is based on the principle of equal access—at home and across Canada—a clear indication to French Canadians that they are welcome everywhere in Canada... The need for an Official Languages Act was one of the major conclusions of the B&B Commission (Royal Commission on Bilingualism and Biculturalism) and we endorsed it in our electoral platform. Prime Minister Trudeau fought an election on this principle: Handle Quebec, yes, but equality of language too. He said the same thing right across Canada and received a mandate from all parts of Canada—no surprises.

I believe that the principle of linguistic equality is accepted by the majority of Canadians, and by an overwhelming majority of young Canadians. When it comes to the Official Languages bill, I think that the so called opposition to the bill comes from a lack of understanding of its main provisions.

This bill specifically provides that the two languages are the official languages of Canada for all purposes of the Parliament and the Government of Canada. It seeks to give to the two languages, in federal matters, an equality of status and equal rights and privileges to their use... Following this general statement of principle, the bill lays down certain requirements respecting documents issued to the public by the government, legislative instruments and decisions of both judicial bodies. The aim is to ensure publication in both languages, wherever possible, at the same time... there is the concept that there must be equal access to the services of the federal government, independently of the language spoken, be it French or English...

I recognize the difficulties in the application of the bill in western Canada... I discussed it with the four western Attorneys General in Victoria... we went through the bill clause by clause. Our position is flexible in terms of detail; but firmly committed in principle... I will try to persuade my cabinet colleagues next week that certain amendments in detail will make the bill more acceptable to western Canadians without sacrificing the principle of the bill...

For those who believe this bill creates a new class of second class citizens; that those who are neither of English or French stock are excluded from full citizenship—my answer is: There is only one class of citizen in Canada. Most of those who have come to Canada have learned to express themselves in French or English. They have not given up their own culture but have lived their lives in opting for one of the two languages and cultures which they found in Canada. Bilingualism does not deprive them of their cultures...

(Nor does it) bar western Canadians from the Federal public service... Much fear (has been) expressed that if this bill were to be enacted, it would (mean) that the Public Service would become the preserve of French-speaking Canadians... Therefore, it is not necessary that a candidate be already bilingual to obtain a position within the public service... however, this policy makes it mandatory that any candidate indicates his willingness to learn the other language at public expense... As for myself, I believe that a national recruitment is a must for national unity and I will not support any policy that could limit public service recruitment to one of two Canadian provinces...

The concept of bilingualism is that of a bilingual state and society rather that a state and society in which every individual is bilingual. In other words, we do not require that every individual be required to speak and write a second language, but rather that each citizen can communicate or deal with the federal government or any of its agents in either of the two official languages—the principle of equal access to the services and institutions of government.

This policy will need a nation's commitment—first it will need the commitment of those of us who speak the English language. We need to make a reasonable accommodation. We need to exercise patience and tolerance. We need to wrestle with our own prejudices... to try to understand with positive goodwill and an open heart.

And it will demand a positive commitment from French Canada, particularly French speaking Canadians living in Quebec. (They must)... make a declared commitment for Canada and a forthright collective decision in favour of Confederation. Western Canadians will be prepared to demonstrate the necessary goodwill if the purpose is a more united Canada, but rightly expect that this faith in our country is reciprocated in Quebec. Unity is a two way street.

We can solve our difficulties. We can reconcile our views... Let us quicken the fashioning of a new nation of two languages so that we can move on to the harvesting of the promise that brought most of us to these shores; where we are, and shall remain one of the most fortunate countries on the face of the earth.

FROM AN ARTICLE IN *TORONTO LIFE*, AUGUST, 1981

In John Turner's description of his family's harrowing adventure down the white water of the Burnside river across the Arctic circle, he wrote:

> I really became a Canadian when I got to know Canada north of the 60th parallel... again we had survived the test of the North. We had shared another unique family experience. Together we had escaped into the Northern frontier and we had survived... what a privilege it was to have run these waters alone... we had traveled one of the last frontiers of the world... I have never felt more Canadian than when alone with my thoughts in the remote northern vastness.

From Chairman's Remarks, Eric Morse Dinner
2 December 1983 – Ottawa, Ontario

This is a unique occasion. We are here to celebrate a man who has elevated canoeing in this country to an art form. Eric Morse pioneered recreational canoeing in our barren lands. For the past sixty-five years he has added to our knowledge of our waterways and of the original explorers and voyageurs who traversed our lakes, rivers and remote lands on their way to discovering our country.

Those who know Eric, or have known him, admire his sense of detail, his endurance, his skill with the paddle. As Sigurd Olson—the great Minnesotan authority on some of his early trips—put it, "He has been an historian by training, but a voyageur by choice."

Eric has traveled most of the three thousand miles of the Great Route from Montreal to Fort Chipewyan. He pioneered the painstaking search of records and diaries of Alex Mackenzie, Peter Pond, David Thompson, Sir John Franklin, Samuel Hearn and George Simpson.

Eric has canoed most of our major Canadian rivers and more particularly the sub-arctic rivers of the Northwest Territories. Each summer starting in 1950, through the sixties and seventies, his canoe trips retraced the early fur trade and early explorers' canoe routes...

He has lectured widely and written extensively in books, articles and papers about the explorers and voyageurs of our Canadian wilderness... What brings us all together is the inspiration he has given all of us and the example he has set during almost three generations for the young people of our country. Only those of us who have paddled the wilderness waters of North America can truly understand why we are here.

Can we evoke for ourselves tonight the memories of a silent paddle on still waters, the slowly evolving landscape of tree and rock and tundra, the easy rhythm of our thought as the paddle cleaves the water, the exhilaration of running rapids, the pain of the portage and, above all, the companionship at the campsite...

The American philosopher, Thoreau, put it succinctly when he wrote: "in wilderness is the salvation of mankind." It must have been an exhilarating experience to canoe with Eric and to be awakened every morning by his cry: "levi, levi, levi nos gens," the traditional morning summons of the early voyageurs. Whether we have canoed with him or not, he has made our lives much richer by his example and his leadership.

1990 Liberal Leadership Convention: John Turner's Farewell

From a Speech to delegates
21 June 1990 – Calgary, Alberta

Twenty-eight years ago, almost to the day, I won back the riding of St. Lawrence–St. George in Montreal for the Liberal party (on 18 June 1962), a party that stood for the kind of Canada I believe in. Twenty-eight years later, it is our party—and our party alone—that still stands for the kind of Canada I believe in. It is our good fortune as Canadians to live in the most beautiful country on earth. It has been our good sense over the generations which has made this country one of the freest and most open democracies in the world. And it has been this great party that has been the most progressive voice for reform throughout the history of our country...

Because Liberals care about what happens to our fellow Canadians. Liberals care that thousands of our fellow Canadians have to line up on a daily basis at food banks for a bag of groceries for themselves and for their families. Liberals care that far too many Canadians are homeless and out on the street. Liberals care that too many Canadians are out of work looking for a job. Liberals care that too many of our Native people are falling victim to despair.

Liberals care that too many of our youth are losing hope in the future. If in this country we don't make education and training a priority once again, and do it fast, the next generation of Canadians will not have the opportunities that we had.

Over the last six years, across Canada and in Parliament, we have fought those who would abandon the disadvantaged in Canada and leave them to their own devices. Whether it was the attack on the universality of our social programs, or the de-indexing of old age pensions, or the reduction of family allowances, or the deconstruction of the unemployment insurance program, or cutbacks in funding for education, or the imposition of unprecedented levels of new and unfair taxation, Liberals were there to lead the fight right across the country.

We fought those battles because we know those policies would lead to a different kind of Canada. Not the kind of Canada our ancestors dreamed of. Not the kind of Canada our grandparents worked so hard to build, but a Canada governed by the politics of greed, where more and more Canadians would not be able to provide themselves and their families with even the basic necessities of life. That is not my vision of Canada. That is not your vision of Canada...

It is through you, my friends, that I have had the opportunity that few Canadians have had, to know our country intimately from coast to coast to coast.

My Canadian 'images' (include)... A salmon barbecue with the Haida people at Hotspring Island in the Queen Charlotte Islands; sailing off the Gulf Islands; the glorious celebration that was the Winter Olympics, here in Calgary; canoeing down the Burnside River to Bathurst Inlet on the Arctic Ocean; meeting with loggers in Kenora in the Rainy River District of Ontario; cheering for the Blue Jays at the Sky Dome; seeing new aluminum being poured at Bagotville on the shores of the Saguenay; walking the fishing ports of Atlantic Canada; supper at harvest time in southern Saskatchewan... and I remember, in the southern part of the great province, these short lines:

> God comes down in the rain,
> And the crop will grow tall
> This is the country faith,
> And the best of all.

You saw that debate (in 1988) on trade. Nothing made my return to public life more worthwhile than being in that debate. Everything I said in the debate I meant, because I believe in Canada. I believe in this country. I believe that we are unique. I believe that we Canadians are different. I believe we have something worth preserving and worth fighting for. I believe that just as a majority of Canadians agreed with me then, an even greater majority agree with me now.

In this country, we are living in some difficult days. I urge you not to let the emotions of the moment, for the next few days (The Meech Lake Accord deadline for ratification was 23 June 1990), cloud our vision of Canada as a strong, independent, sovereign, and above all united country.

Over the past few months Canadians have spoken passionately about their views of Canada, and how their views should be reflected in our Constitution... We must never give up on this country, never, never, never, never!

I watched as you did; Canadians are almost unanimous in the belief that the recent marathon negotiating session in Ottawa was wrong. Our Constitution is a national contract. It is our national bond. Changing it requires public scrutiny, open debate, frank and critical analysis, all this leading to public understanding.

I hope that we have now learned that the people must be involved in this process, and to do that the process must be public... As the talks went on and on, Canadians waited, feeling frustrated, feeling helpless. After all, this was our country they were talking about. After all, this was our future they were talking about. And we were not even there and we couldn't even see or hear what was going on!...

There are going to be scars. Together we must work on healing the wounds that have been opened, the wounds that have been opened up by this debate. We have somehow to rekindle the great spirit which brought this country together 123 years ago. The flame of nationhood must be relit. The mood of tolerance regained. The confidence in ourselves restored.

All Canadians, not just in this great forum, not just Liberals, but all Canadians want to see this country succeed. Our forefathers built a nation from sea to sea to sea. We settled half a continent; we prospered as have few other nations on the face of the earth. Talk to the people of Eastern Europe! We are the envy of the world. We grew in tolerance and understanding and we grew in wealth and security. Now we again have a task to reestablish the national unity of a great country.

In these very crucial, critical and sensitive days for Canada, I would like all of us to remember the spirit of generosity and the common bonds which hold us together as a nation. And remember also, words that come to my mind from Shakespeare's *Henry V*:

Combine your hearts in one, your realms in one!
That English may as French, French Englishmen
Receive each other!

If we are to meet this challenge, this national challenge, we need to call on the best and the brightest of the next generation to take an active role with us in the political like of this country. We need more people who are willing to set aside, for a time, their own personal goals and put the country first.

As I said to you and others six years ago, we need to welcome more people into this party who are willing to do that. My pledge was to open up this party to new ideas, new people, new approaches. I promised you a more open party. We are a more open party. I promised you a more democratic party. We are now more democratic. I promised you a more accountable party. We are now more accountable. Our party again belongs to you. Make sure it stays that way!...

I believe that the highest calling in life, next to the Ministry of God, is public office. It has given me the opportunity to return a little of what our country has given to me. You are part of the system too. We cannot take our public process for granted. We cannot always leave it to others. We have a great country that is worth preserving. That won't happen unless more people care—care about Canada—and unless more people are willing to do something about it.

Of course, public service can at times be rough—Geills and I ought to know. From the bottom of my heart, I want to thank her and my family, every one of them, for their understanding and their support, in good days and bad days. Those of us in public life can fight back, but families can't fight back. In public life there are no secrets. Your life becomes an open book, subject to a thousand different interpretations, speculation and insinuation. It comes with the territory.

I say to my colleagues in the House of Commons and the Senate, and in the legislatures across our great country—what a magnificent territory it is!

One of the proudest moments in my life was the day I was first sworn in as a Member of Parliament. My proudest boast today is that I am the Member of Parliament for Vancouver Quadra.

It is a humbling experience to be given the trust of one's fellow citizens, one's constituents to represent them in the highest court in the land—Parliament. Parliament ensures that all voices are heard. It is at the heart of our democracy. No government at any level can be allowed to ignore the rights of Members of Parliament or members of a legislature, because in so doing, they are ignoring your rights too and they are ignoring the rights of every Canadian.

I have fought for my vision of Canada. My dream has always been that one day we would live up to the promise of Sir Wilfrid Laurier and fulfill that great potential we have as a nation.

We have such a unique heritage, such boundless opportunity. Our limitless land, water, resources. Our northern frontier. The space to be alone when you want to. Our two languages, many cultures. Our spirit of freedom and tolerance. Our respect for the law. Our faith in Parliamentary democracy.

We want this nation to endure because millions of Canadians share my dream for a Canada that is strong, independent, sovereign and united.

If I have helped concentrate the attention of Canadians on these issues, if I have helped focus our national purpose, if I have managed to encourage only a few others to become involved, then my time will have been well spent.

Chapter 6

John Turner's Federalism

John Turner's personal roots—and later elected ones as well—in Quebec, British Columbia and Ontario, more than qualified him to play a leading role on the public stage when changes in Quebec society, known as the Quiet Revolution, burst into the forefront of Canadian consciousness. Even before his work in politics, observing and participating, as a lawyer in Montreal in the 1950s, he gained experience that qualified him, like few other English speakers outside Quebec, to later speak out on issues of Canadian federalism and unity.

"Any discussion of Canadian unity must begin with the realistic acceptance of one basic fact: that the province of Quebec is different from all the other provinces of Canada," he told an English-speaking audience in 1968 when at 38, he ran for party leader. "This fact must be recognized. A refusal to do so, a denial of this *situation de fait* could lead to the separation of Quebec from Canada. And politicians must face the facts."

And face facts he did.

In 1987, Turner experienced one of the greatest challenges of his career when the Meech Lake Accord was agreed to by Canada's First Ministers. With Pierre Trudeau's vision of Canada so heavily entrenched in his party, the easy course to chart would have been in opposing the Accord, scoring political points along the way. He did no such thing. Turner embraced the Accord as a first step in recognizing what he'd seen with his own eyes, from his extensive reading of history, and from what he'd learned in both the 1950s and 1960s. He courageously supported the Accord and its call for Quebec's recognition as a distinct society. He never wavered in this support over the next three years, despite the very public opposition to Meech that galvanized and split many Liberals after Trudeau had bravely intervened against it.

In 1992 and as a private Member of the Commons, Turner gave a powerful address in defence of the Charlottetown Accord:

> In my view, those who opposed Meech Lake will bear the burden of history for the national disruption of the last three exasperating years, lost opportunities, a gnawing national frustration and who knows what permanent damage to the psyche of the country. I have never, in 30 years since being elected to the House of Commons, had trouble as a Canadian, certainly as a former Member of Parliament from Quebec, with the concept of a distinct society. For me it reflects reality. A different majority language, a different system of law, a different history, a different culture, different traditions, and a different sense of humour.

He then ended his last major address in the Commons:

> Let us reassert our belief in ourselves as a nation, using the words of Laurier, "great among the nations of the world." We are the envy of the world. It is time we woke up. It is time we shook ourselves out of this lethargy. I hope that this national debate encourages all of us, all Canadians, to stand up, to speak up strongly and loudly and clearly for Canada. I support the motion and I will campaign for it.

Consistency on the greatest issue of all, Canada's unity, is Turner's legacy.

Arthur Milnes

Off the Couch and Back to the Drawing Board

21 October 1964 – Vancouver, British Columbia

Each visit to Vancouver is a homecoming for me. For 15 years I have been exiled in that remote part of the country on the other side of the mountains. It is good to return to the promised land...

I remember during our university days how optimistic we were. I can still see the billboards proclaiming "British Columbia has men to match her mountains." That is hardly an exaggeration. One thing has not changed since I left. It is that buoyant, confident spirit which is the distinguishing mark of British Columbians.

But one thing has changed. Another ingredient has been added to this buoyancy, this optimism. There is a feeling here that goes beyond self-reliance. It is an attitude that approaches "we can go it alone." Ottawa be damned! Ottawa seems very remote from Vancouver. This is not entirely new. (It used to be said that) while it is 2,800 miles from Vancouver to Ottawa, it was 28,000 from Ottawa to Vancouver! On this visit I sense a self-confident feeling—that BC may be able to do without the rest of the country. I sense the illusion of a new kingdom of the West.

This is typical of Canadians. British Columbians will never admit that there is anything wrong with the West Coast. Albertans don't knock Alberta. People in Ontario talk about their province as if civilization ended at the Manitoba boundary. Quebecers have a passion for La Belle Province. Maritimers are again talking about an Atlantic union. When we look at Canada in regional terms, Canadians are not frightened, confused or unhappy. In fact, everyone seems to be satisfied to the verge of smugness with where he lives.

But we hear people in the east asking what is British Columbia up to? People on the Prairies criticize Toronto. Toronto is suspicious of Montreal, and there are some people in Quebec who mutter darkly about English Canadian plots. But nobody's dissatisfied with himself. There is even one thing that everyone agrees about—Ottawa is fair game for criticism. It sometimes seems that Ottawa is 28,000 miles from everywhere.

It disturbs me that Canadians are still thinking regionally after almost 100 years. I am concerned that people in British Columbia may be thinking in terms of the West Coast rather than in terms of Canada, or that people in Quebec may be putting Quebec first, Canada second. I am concerned, as many of us are, about the Canadian identity, about the Canadian fact of nationhood. The tide of regionalism in Canada is everywhere on the flood. Centrifugal forces, regionally expressed, are at play—tending to fracture the country and to leave a vacuum at the core. It was surely these regional forces which provoked two successive minority governments in Canada (1962 under John Diefenbaker, 1963 under Lester B. Pearson). People voted geographically: the West against the East, the cities and suburbia against the towns and the rural areas. Neither major party was able to muster enough support nationally from each region in the country to gain a majority of the seats in the House of Commons. This has made strong federal governments more difficult, because Canadians have not been reacting as a nation.

Many Canadians are disturbed about this trend. They are troubled about the whittling down of federal power and the transfer of influence from Ottawa to provincial capitals. This is the vital issue today. How can we maintain a national voice in a noisy climate of regionalism? How in this day when provincial governments are reasserting their historic rights and responsibilities in such a convincing fashion, do we hold the nation together? What is the new role of the federal government? That is the crucial question.

Let us accept the present trend toward decentralization as a political fact... so let us face facts: we must be realistic. But we don't have to be pessimistic. Historically, Canadians have seen before cycles of influence shifting between Ottawa and the provinces. In periods of crisis, depression or war, power flows to Ottawa, while in more stable times, the provinces reclaim that power. Under the national policy of Sir John A. Macdonald we fell under the centralist influence: power was concentrated in Ottawa. Then, during the years of the Watson-Haldane decisions of the Privy Council until the mid-30s, the forces pulled the other way, and the power of the federal government was steadily curtailed to the advantage of the provinces. Then came the Rowell-Sirois Commission report. The pressures of the depression and the war and the post-war reconstruction years reversed the trend and swung us again towards strong federal government. What we are witnessing today in Canada is a natural counter-reaction to this past generation of increasing central power.

Decentralization is not necessarily a bad thing. Some areas of government are better managed closer to the people—by the provinces. Some aspects of our life are better handled from Ottawa. Every federal state is constantly in flux. There is a perpetual ebb and flow of political forces between the central and provincial governments. In the US the doctrine of states' rights has been recurring importance. It is an issue today in the American election. What is important for us Canadians to remember is that the present flow of power away from Ottawa is not necessarily inflexible nor eternal.

Regionalism, therefore, is not a mystery, nor is it unknown to our history: it is a by-product of decentralization. But today, more than the normal cyclical pressures are at play. The present needs of our people have called for a larger role for the provincial governments—a role more important than was originally foreseen at the time of Confederation. The needs of a modern society have called for an increase in the public sector of the economy. Most of the pressing and urgent needs of Canadians fall today within fields of provincial jurisdiction: education, roads, urban development and renewal, the taming and tapping of our natural resources—these are all provincial matters. To fulfill these responsibilities towards the Canadian people, the provinces need money. Because Canadians have made these matters the priorities of today, the provinces are obtaining a larger share of the public purse. It makes sense that the government which has the responsibility for spending should have the authority to collect the tax and be responsible for that share of the tax load.

It is within this general context of regionalism that we must view the present situation in Quebec. The renaissance in Quebec is to some extent but another expression of regionalism. In a larger sense, it is the awakening of a people who were one of the original and equal partners in our Confederation. The powers and revenues that Quebec requires for the cultural and economic emancipation of French Canada are the same forces that other provinces are demanding for the fulfilment of their own responsibilities. The basic cry of *Maîtres chez nous*—masters in our own house—is echoed in varying degrees in every province in Canada. The slogans may be different; the requirements are surprisingly similar. Every province is seeking its own place in the sun.

What the provincial politicians may be forgetting, of course, is that it is still we the Canadian people who are involved. The people have very little patience with jurisdictional squabbles. The individual citizen does not care if the road he walks on, the school he sends his children to, the health or pension plan which protects his family— he or she doesn't care if these items are financed by the provincial or federal treasury. In either event his or her share of the cost will be taken out of his annual income. No matter who administers, the citizen pays. Most English-speaking Canadians approach the matter with this type of Anglo-Saxon pragmatism—the feeling of "let's get the job done." But we run the temptation that we might not recognize that, for the French-speaking Canadian, this pragmatic approach is not enough. He wants a clear recognition and respect under the constitution for the proposition that those ingredients of his material welfare upon which his cultural identity depends must be handled by the province.

What is happening in Quebec? French-speaking Canadians are seeking a new climate of self-fulfilment. The people of Quebec want to make up for lost time. They are Canadians in a hurry. The French-speaking Canadian, in economic terms, slept for generations. Now he is awake. Now he is impatient to catch up. He has a craving for education and for skills and competence of every kind. He has an urge for material improvement and wants to develop Quebec. He seeks to fulfill himself in his own language whether for his bread and butter or for his leisure. He seeks a new tone of political maturity. For French-speaking Canadians the so-called "quiet revolution" is not a revolution against Canada; it is a revolution against themselves.

The very real measure of accomplishment in Quebec during the past four years has been scarred and blurred by the harsh voices and irrational acts of a few. We must expect this. In any movement of such depth and momentum, we must expect some instability. But we do not have to let ourselves be blackmailed by separatists. The vast majority of French Canadians reject separatism. They are looking for an economically emancipated Quebec within a more vibrant Canada. They want the powers and revenues to develop Quebec according to their own pressing priorities. They want the right to use and cultivate their own language and culture. They want to be as Canadian as you or I. In short, they seek recognition of the equal partnership in Confederation. If we English-speaking Canadians, on our part, reject this partnership, reject the idea of a dual culture in Canada, then we reject the possibility of a viable Canadian nation. I am convinced that most Canadians understand the basis of our confederation and believe it can work. We need to remember that moderation must speak in both languages. We must repudiate separatists of either language—those who counsel that we can go it alone.

A Canadian who thinks in terms of only a regional loyalty is at fault, he is less a Canadian no matter which language he speaks. A French-speaking Canadian who thinks solely in terms of Quebec is no more dangerous for the future of this country than the British Columbian who cannot see beyond the mountains. Decentralization is a political fact; regionalism is its potential result. What is more dangerous for Canada to my mind than a decentralizing of power is the decentralizing of feeling—this fracturing of a national emotion, this loyalty toward provincial aspirations rather than towards the national interest. This country, after all, as the prime minister said before this club only a month ago, is greater than the sum of its parts. Loyalty to a province must not undermine pride of a nation.

There is a basic interdependence between the various parts of our country. British Columbia is an exporting province. This is true. This province makes a great contribution to the Canadian balance of payments and to the Canadian economy. But this doesn't make the province economically self-sufficient. British Columbia needs markets and our trading partners abroad will only buy from us if they can sell to us. They will only buy from British Columbia if they can sell to Ontario and Quebec. BC's trade depends on the rest of Canada. A trade is a two-way street. There is another point. As the manufacturing potential of British Columbia grows, the market in the rest of Canada will be even more important to you. The unit costs determined by a market of two million people would never allow British Columbia as a separate power to compete against the world—a world where larger and larger trading units and customs unions are now being formed. It is to the central government that we must look to create the climate for the growth and prosperity of each province.

There is another important reason for the new look in the provinces. Growing power in the provinces is reflected by the growing ambition of men in provincial capitals. Politics is more than principles, more than issues. Politics is people. Never before in our history have so many strong personalities been lodged at the same time in all our provincial capitals. These men have access to all the techniques of electronic communication. Television has been the great equalizer in politics. In Canada it allows a provincial premier or a mayor to challenge a Canadian prime minister. Before the camera everyone starts even. It is not surprising, therefore, that the Canadian people have been influenced by such a concentration of energy and willpower in our provincial capitals. Ten strong provincial premiers are competing for national attention.

How have we responded as a nation to this trend of decentralization? How have we reacted? We have brooded. We have put ourselves on a collective couch. We have subjected ourselves to endless self-analysis. We have wondered out loud about the Canadian identity. We have asked ourselves whether the price of being Canadian is still worth paying for. Soul searching has become a national disease.

What is the remedy? What must we do? The first thing we have to do is to get off the couch and back to the drawing board. Less brooding, more action. Less analyzing, more living. More living of the Canadian fact. An identity is not conjured up, it is lived. It is not rationalized, it is felt. Just as a doctor fulfills himself not by questioning himself or asking himself what he is, but by practising medicine, so Canadians will build an identity for themselves and their children by living as Canadians. Canada is not a concept in the air. Canada is the collective identity of all those who fulfill this everyday living of the Canadian fact. After all, most of us live in this country because we want to be Canadians.

We have suffered as a nation because we have lost our youthful vigour. Our momentum has slackened. Yet no (other) people in the world have such a future. Nowhere are men and women so fortunate. There is so much to be done in this land: so much wealth to be discovered, so many resources to be tapped, so much to be built. There is enough to be done in Canada to give each one of us enough to do for a lifetime. Let's go at it with zest and enthusiasm. Instead of reacting defensively to the problem of unity, let us attack our common purpose around which all of us can unite by the very process of achieving it. We have common goals; and we have the problems common to the 20th century that should unite us: how to cope in the nuclear age, how to live in a world of immediate communication, how to adjust to automation and the computer, how to eliminate unemployment in an age of growing productivity, how to increase our skills, how to enjoy leisure time.

This country can again become a nation of builders—building a mid-20th century Canada. We have a wealth of resources to exploit and harness on a national scale. We have our forests, our soil, our water, our people. We have the unlimited treasures of the North. What better forum than this confident, buoyant province to make a plan for a new optimism in Canada, a new optimism that will dissipate cynicism and brooding, an optimism based not solely on dreams or visions but on the excitement of daily accomplishment.

I am talking about optimism on a national scale—an optimism as determined and far-sighted for our time as that of the fathers of Confederation a century ago. We must weave the fabric of a new national policy from the strands of our common interests as they exist for us in the environment of the second half of the 20th century.

This policy must, of course, be achieved within the framework of our constitution. The federal government is limited by having only a joint jurisdiction over resources, agriculture, welfare and taxation. But here is where cooperative federalism can become a positive force. What is this doctrine of cooperative federalism? It is nothing more nor less than a recognition of the interdependence of governments in a federal state. It is government by prior consultation and coordination in fields of common jurisdiction. The federal government can achieve national leadership and a national policy by bringing the other jurisdictions together under common programmes. Ottawa can achieve a national policy by bringing provincial heads together: national leadership by persuasion, not dictation. Provincial boundaries mean less today than they did yesterday. Government policy is contagious. What is done in one province affects another, and the problems facing every province are common to all.

The catch-phrases of provincial self-sufficiency are misleading. They disguise the underlying reality that what has been achieved at the provincial level has been made possible because of national trade and fiscal policies. What we have achieved locally has been made possible by the national environment.

Given the fiscal resources to fulfill their own responsibilities, the provinces must recognize that cooperative federalism is a two-way street. Provincial government has its responsibilities, yes; but federal government has its responsibilities too: responsibilities important for all Canadians. The provinces must not impinge upon the federal sphere. Ottawa must not be a vacuum—it must be a focus—a focus for the whole country. Within its own exclusive jurisdiction—fiscal and monetary policy, trade and commerce, banking, foreign affairs and defence—the federal government can press on unfettered to a strong and imaginative programme.

A national policy for Canada does not mean the repudiation of provincial rights and aspirations. It does not invade the provincial jurisdiction. It recognizes the interdependence of governments, but it assumes the interdependence of people everywhere in this country upon each other. The historic urge that brought the several colonies in British North America to a common destiny still applies: that we can do better together than we can separately. The logic of that national urge makes even more sense today. Twenty million people can do better than 2 million, and 50 million would do better than 20 million.

Let us live then as Canadians. Let us become builders, once again, of a nation, in mid-20th century terms. We can find our Canadian identity by living as Canadians, not by brooding on a couch. We will not, thereby, be denying our provincial loyalties. A British Columbian or Quebecois does not cease being a good Canadian because he advances the legitimate interests of his own province. But he will be helping his province more in an interdependent world if his priorities and hopes are attached to the future of his country first and foremost—if he is Canadian first and always.

Quebec Is Different

From a Speech to Hamilton Liberals

26 March 1968 – Hamilton, Ontario

Any discussion of Canadian unity must begin with the realistic acceptance of one basic fact: that the province of Quebec is different from all the other provinces of Canada. This has always been a fact—a political fact in Canadian life. Quebec is a province which represents approximately 80 percent of one of our two major linguistic groups. They are all descendants of 60,000 who came from France, settled in Northern America and called themselves *Canadiens*. The overwhelming majority of French-speaking citizens of the province of Quebec share a distinctive, philosophical and cultural background. They share a pride in their unique history of survival in North America. They share a sense of nationalism different from all the other provinces. Quebec is governed through a system of law different from both the British common law system and the French legal system. In reality, therefore,

Quebec is different! This fact must be recognized. A refusal to do so, a denial of this situation *de fait* could lead to the separation of Quebec from Canada. And politicians must face the facts.

The attitude of the province of Quebec has varied from the attitude of other provinces in the first century of Canada. Prior to 1960, Quebec maintained a defensive position with respect to its rights. While English Canada has looked to Ottawa for leadership, the province of Quebec has looked to Quebec City for protection. Quebec hid behind a curtain of isolation, a refusal to enter a dialogue with the rest of Canada. Quebec's attitude has changed. It is now essentially positive. Since 1960, I have found in Quebec a renewal of pride, a desire for competence and an unprecedented urge to control its own destiny.

Today, in 1968, Quebec is no longer satisfied with the present situation. It claims, as do other provinces, that its powers under the British North America Act are not sufficient to cope with the rising demands of a modern, urban society. The building of new roads, new schools, new hospitals and new homes, already overtax the existing fiscal capacities of our provincial and municipal governments. While these responsibilities have expanded, their resources have remained the same. Furthermore, Quebec feels that the federal government has only recently taken an initiative in promoting the dual nature of our country—that the federal government has only recently reacted to the fact that 30 percent of all Canadian citizens speak the French language.

Quebec feels much has to be done. For example, in our foreign policy, have we reflected the bilingual and bicultural personality of Canada? Have we used our experience in the British Commonwealth to forge a similar community of the French-speaking people?

Is there really equal opportunity between English and French speaking citizens of our country? Bilingualism is just one test. Do citizens of Canada, who are only French-speaking, have the same opportunity to become senior officials of the federal government as a citizen who speaks only English? We all know the answer to that! It is clear that the crisis in Canada will not be resolved through mere translation. It will be resolved through a hard negotiation aimed at a system of equal opportunity for all Canadians.

Quebec feels, rightly or wrongly, that the federal government has been against change—that we in English Canada have vested interest in the status quo.

In the past, whenever the question of the exercise of powers between the federal government and the provinces has arisen, English Canada has said, "Let Ottawa do it," while Quebec has said, "Why can't the provinces do it themselves?"

This explains why English Canada and Quebec have approached constitutional questions from opposite poles. We must bridge this gap by hard negotiation. And by hard negotiation, I do not mean confrontation.

If we are sincere in our stated position that we are not afraid of change, negotiations in good faith on all sides must begin—and within the next few months. Otherwise, many in Quebec will continue to feel "Confederation if necessary, but not necessarily Confederation."

Two problems therefore confront national unity:

1. To resolve the language problem in Canada.

2. To reassess the division of powers between the federal and provincial governments. The French-English aspect of this problem has recently made progress toward a solution. The last constitutional conference in Ottawa, and the earlier work in Toronto demonstrated to all Canadians that the solution to these problems are attainable, if our approach is realistic, and conducted in a positive atmosphere.

It is clear that if French Canada cannot feel at home throughout the length and breadth of Canada, it is inevitable that French Canadians will withdraw within the borders of Quebec, under subterfuge of "associate statehood."

To allow French Canadians to participate in the mainstream of our society throughout the whole of our country, we must expand French linguistic rights across the whole of our country. This linguistic expansion can only enrich the total Canadian society.

Our youth know this. We, the parents, still resist this idea. But let's not fool ourselves. We must take this positive approach.

How else can we work towards making French Canada more a part of Canada? In my opinion, where there is a French-speaking minority, government services at both federal and provincial levels and education must be made in French. Television and radio networks must be extended throughout the country. To my mind, these are minimum requirements for a united country.

The second aspect of the problem is even more crucial. How do we reshape the constitutional powers to keep pace with modern demands?

Here, the province of Quebec has been more vocal than the others because of its historic interest in preserving its cultural autonomy, but all provinces are now interested in a new, fresh distribution of powers.

We have agreed to hold a series of federal–provincial meetings on constitutional problems at the working level. We must mobilize the best brains in Canada to participate. We must bring from business, from the universities, from labour, from our parliamentary backbench and from the opposition, the men and women of talent who can contribute to an effective reshaping of our constitution. The solution to the most important issue of our times must not be found in a closed shop.

We need a permanent secretariat, representative of all governments, constantly in operation, until a new draft constitution has been prepared for the decisions of government. Such machinery for a constitutional revision should cover the entire field and include all the implications of change in the economic, the social, the legal as well as political areas and we should operate continuously until a new document relevant to our times can be produced for decision.

Throughout this process, the attitude of the federal government should be firm, yet flexible. Firm because the federal government must retain levers to manage and control economic opportunity and fiscal integrity for all Canada. In that sense, the economic viability of Canada is the limit to any negotiation. Once the question of an essential economic and fiscal power has been settled, we can be flexible and negotiate all areas. Our object is to build a new federalism that works effectively and efficiently in the best interest of a new Canada geared to the modern world.

The obstacle to constitutional change is the fear that we will become unable to manage and plan the national economy. Constitutional changes can be a means, however, of improving the federal government's ability to stimulate growth, fight inflation and recessions and raise the dispossessed regions of Canada.

This means that Ottawa must retain complete control of national monetary and fiscal policies. Ottawa must retain a sufficient tax base to fight inflation and recession. These powers are now at the federal level and will have to be made more effective.

At the moment, more than two-thirds of government expenditures made in Canada are spent at the provincial and federal levels. To strengthen the positions of the federal government on economic and fiscal matters, new institutions for consultation and coordination are now required. For example, the federal government, managing the money supply and fixing taxes, can see its efforts frustrated by an immediate increase in provincial taxes. Any regulation of the money supply must take into account capital needs at all levels of government. This requires foreknowledge of provincial programmes and of expenditure.

The federal government should retain its initiative in fiscal and economic matters and, furthermore, increase its fiscal and monetary ability by coordinating the exercise by all governments of their exclusive and concurrent powers. We need a permanent intergovernment secretariat for economic and fiscal matters.

A major role of new federalism will be to raise the dispossessed regions of Canada, to make opportunity equal for all Canadians. We must destroy the special status of those who are poor. This implies the right of the federal government to equalize revenues between provinces, to raise money by way of taxation to achieve this equalization of opportunities.

The approach of the federal government in any negotiation is all important. Some start from the position that all provinces are the same. I say that this is closing our eyes to political reality. Theories are fine but of no use if they don't work. I want a new federalism that works.

Flexibility does not imply weakness. A fixed position does not imply strength. Once a strong economic and political Canada is assured, the negotiation of power between the federal and provincial governments can proceed in good faith. From there we start with a clause by clause examination of powers under the *British North America Act*. In these negotiations, some powers will be expanded, some will be diminished, some will be exchanged. Any fresh allocation of powers will be settled by one test: where they work best in the interest of all our citizens. To illustrate, as minister responsible for administration of the *Bankruptcy Act*, I negotiated with the province of Quebec an agreement which would allow federal prosecutors to go into Quebec to enforce the *Bankruptcy Act*. This has worked.

Social security should be gradually transferred to provincial administration. I do not believe that such a change would weaken the federal government's ability to control the national economy. The cost of welfare and service is a fixed and continuing cost. It cannot be increased or reduced as a device to fight against short-term economic trends.

Similarly, under a new division of powers, provinces should have the right to negotiate international agreements with respect to matters falling under their jurisdiction. Negotiated under the auspices of the federal government, such a treaty would be automatically signed by the federal government unless it is contrary to Canada's overall foreign policy objectives.

A new redistribution of powers should also empower the provincial governments to establish their own TV and radio networks provided that all technical control is maintained by the federal government to prevent anarchy on their airwaves. This is not to say that the Canadian Broadcasting Corporation or Radio Canada should be turned over to provincial administration and control. To the contrary, Canada must retain and expand a bilingual television and radio network from coast to coast and over the territories.

Under a fresh distribution of powers, Ottawa might be responsible for pollution control, auto safety, and a national resource policy. These and other areas can now be best handled at the federal level. The important thing is that we should approach all negotiations with an open mind—without rigid preconceptions or historic prejudices. I believe that with this positive approach we can settle the vexing problems challenging this generation of Canadians.

The Meech Lake Accord
From a speech to the House of Commons
1 May 1987 – Ottawa, Ontario

I first want to congratulate the Prime Minister of Canada (Mr. Mulroney) as well as Quebec Premier Robert Bourassa and the other provincial premiers for their constructive work and the result achieved yesterday. It is a happy day for Canada and for Quebec, particularly for all those who believed that our country would remain united by respecting the diversity of its regions and the equality of its citizens. I have always believed that it was essential to the future of our country that Quebec be a major and leading partner in the Canadian federation and a full-fledged participant in its evolution.

That is what I stated in an interview with *Le Devoir* in June 1986, and what has led the Liberal Party of Canada to adopt, at its convention last November, a clear position on the place of Quebec within the constitutional agreement of 1982.

I must tell the House that the constructive work of the Liberal Opposition and the New Democratic Party did contribute to create a favourable atmosphere and context for this agreement... we refrained from politicizing this question in the House of Commons. I, as much as the Members of the Official Opposition and the New Democrats purposely avoided embarrassing the government about this issue. We knew that the provincial premiers and the representatives of the Canadian government were studying the views set forth by Quebec, and that it was desirable that the interests of the country take precedence over partisan considerations...

In commending the Prime Minister and his colleagues, the First Ministers of the provinces, I want to say to him that the work accomplished yesterday was encouraging and constructive for the country. Bringing Quebec into our constitutional fabric, fully into the Canadian family, was an effort worth his time and worth the time of the First Ministers.

The Charlottetown Accord

FROM A SPEECH TO THE HOUSE OF COMMONS
10 SEPTEMBER 1992 – OTTAWA, ONTARIO

Mr. Speaker, what the prime minister (Brian Mulroney) characterized as a Canadian compromise is certainly cause for congratulations to the prime minister, and particularly to the minister responsible for Constitutional Affairs (Joe Clark).

Those gentlemen, the leaders of our country, are entitled to bask in the glow of their achievement. For Canadians generally, however, the consensus at Charlottetown is more cause not for congratulations, but for a collective sigh of relief. It is some release from the constitutional fatigue that has been building into a national trauma.

It all began when Quebec was excluded from the 1982 agreement. Reopening the constitutional issue in 1985 might have been a *beau risqué*, to use the words of René Lévèsque cited Tuesday by the prime minister. It was a dangerous risk, too.

Nonetheless, the prime minister did achieve an accord at Meech Lake. It was an accord which, to my view, supported by good constitutional advice from across the country, particularly from the then attorney general of Ontario—Ian Scott, who retired from the legislature early this week—was a satisfactory compromise allowing Quebec its recognition as a distinct society within our Confederation without yielding federal power.

Despite all the assertions to the contrary, there was no sacrifice in that accord of the federal spending power. Indeed, the accord was specific in stating that nothing in that agreement altered in any way the balance between federal and provincial constitutional authority.

Granted, the accord responded primarily to Quebec's concerns, but it would have been a useful first step in the renewal of our Confederation. It was contemplated by all the first ministers, and it was certainly contemplated by the prime minister, that the problem of western alienation and the injustice shown for centuries toward the original peoples would have been addressed thereafter.

I read that document of Meech Lake carefully. I have read the current document just as carefully. Meech Lake was a far cleaner deal than the document we now have before the House. In my view, those who opposed Meech Lake will bear the burden of history for the national disruption of the last three exasperating years; lost opportunities, a gnawing national frustration and who knows what permanent damage to the psyche of the country.

I have always been suspicious of referenda or plebiscites. Of course they are the ultimate democratic gesture. But the more complicated the national fabric of a country, the more divisive a referendum can be. A referendum is simplistic, reducing complex issues to a simple yes or no answer.

Moreover, under our parliamentary system we have representative democracy. In Canada we elect those who sit in the House and in the legislatures, and those who are municipal councillors. We elect those whom we charge or mandate to analyze the issues for us, to vote for us, and we hold them to account regularly at general elections.

A referendum tends to be an abrogation of that process because under our representative democracy we rely on the judgment of our Members of Parliament and members of the legislatures. We rely on their ability, in the best interests of their constituents and of the country generally, to act on our behalf and to vote on our behalf.

A referendum is an abrogation of that style of leadership. It is the quick fix. Having said that, what is done is done and there are provincial referenda in place. Therefore, I accept the fact that we now have a referendum. The people will decide and we will await their ultimate decision. I can tell you it is far from a done deal in many parts of Canada right now.

Looking at the substance of this consensus report from Charlottetown on August 29—I have never in 30 years since being elected to the House of Commons had trouble as a Canadian, certainly as a former Member of Parliament from Quebec, with the concept of a distinct society. For me it reflects reality: a different majority language, a different system of law, a different history, a different culture, different traditions, and a different sense of humour.

It is now more clearly defined in this document. I reiterate what I said in the House once before, which was reconfirmed by the judgment of the late Justice Jean Beetz in the Supreme Court of Canada on the sign language law, that a distinct society in Quebec includes not only a French-speaking majority but it includes the English-speaking minority. This is part of that distinct society. There is no impingement of minority rights by the concept of a distinct society.

Mr. Speaker (John Fraser), in Vancouver, which you and I have the honour to represent, and elsewhere, Quebecers are visiting us this summer, certainly on the Voyageur Program. They must feel pretty good seeing those bumper stickers that say "My Canada Includes Quebec." For me there is no Canada without Quebec.

If I were a Quebecer, I think I would be satisfied with this agreement. It might not be as good as I would have wished, but it is probably better than what I expected...

If I were a Quebecer, this document would provide a better protection for my language, my culture, my heritage, my system of civil law. Quebec's control over its natural resources and immigration is improved, and Quebec is guaranteed a third of the Supreme Court judges and more importantly, 25 percent of the seats in this House, that is to say 25 per cent of the shares in the business that is Canada. It has a perpetual guarantee of 25 percent of the seats in order to protect the home base of French speakers in Canada—Quebec. On top of that it has veto power over any change in federal institutions.

If I were a Quebecer, I would say again: my homeland is Quebec, but my country is Canada.

I salute the justice finally accorded to our first peoples. Finally, recognition of the inherent constitutional rights of our original peoples, the constitutional right to self-government. I want to caution the House that strong leadership is going to be needed from all quarters during the next five years to make it work.

These provisions—the distinct society and the inherent right to self-government for our original peoples—were perhaps what Sir Wilfrid Laurier had in mind when, in this House, he recalled a visit to Canterbury Cathedral in London, a cathedral made of granite, oak and marble. This is what he said to the House:

> It is the image of the nation I wish to see Canada. For here, I want the granite to remain granite, the oak to remain oak, and the marble to remain marble. Out of these elements, I would build a nation great among the nations of the world.

What about the Senate? We argued this issue in this House on a government motion by the then Minister of Justice (John Crosbie), now Minister of Fisheries and Oceans, on 7 June 1985. I remember it, it was my birthday.

At that time I repeated what I had written in a thesis that is now gathering dust in the library at the University of British Columbia, although there is a well worn copy in the Senate library here. The thesis was to the effect that the Senate should be abolished and, if not abolished, elected so that it became a real territorial balance against the overwhelming population of our central provinces.

Now we will have an elected Senate, an improvement certainly for western Canada. We are going to have an equal Senate, as the Leader of the Opposition said on Tuesday, at the price of being a less effective one...

There will be a better equilibrium in our Confederation as the result of an elected Senate, but it is impossible to predict how effective individual senators are going to be under our new parliamentary process. It is impossible to predict the interaction of the two Houses. One thing is certain, the power of the Senate to defeat a bill and then force a joint session of the House of Commons and the Senate will add a new dynamic in the power structure of this country and, frankly, I am optimistic that it can work.

On the issue of division of powers between federal and provincial jurisdictions, I do not believe that the federal authority gave away too much, although I have some doubts about culture, telecommunications and broadcasting and I deplore, as the leader of the Opposition does, the weak economic union clause.

As I said during the trade debate, I have read the document. It is not a perfect document. It is not my document. But it is the only document we have. It happens to be the document resulting from hours and days and months of strenuous negotiations, finally culminating with our democratically elected leaders from every part of the country and every segment of the country agreeing on this consensus. For that reason it deserves our support.

We Canadians ought to recognize that this referendum is more than just a debate about words, laws and powers. It is about the future of our country as a cohesive, emotional, economic union. This debate not only involves our future as a people, but our individual well-being as citizens...

We have been warned by the new political gurus of our age, the omnipotent pollsters, that we should not preach fear in this debate.

Does that mean that we cannot say to our fellow citizens that there are economic consequences of failure for all of us, that we should not warn that dividing up the huge public debt will not be costly, that we should not caution that there will be an effect upon our credit rating in the markets of the world, or upon the exchange rate, or upon interest rates, or that our trade would not be affected, or jobs and investments not lost?

No, this is not an abstract debate. This has real consequences, on a daily basis, for every one of us and every one of our constituents. More important, if we fail, it will affect the way that we feel about ourselves. We will feel that we have let ourselves down. We will feel that we have lost, perhaps irretrievably, the uniqueness we had as a special nation.

Canadians want a positive conclusion to this question. Most of us in this country believe that we have a great and beautiful land. Most of us believe that Canada has been a wonderful experiment. Most of us believe that Canada has been a great achievement. We are reluctant to sing the praises of our country, restrained in our patriotism. Waving the flag is not our way, not our style.

I happen to believe that we need renewal. Certainly we need renewal of our Constitution. We need renewal of our pride in our country.

We need to shed our cynicism and our negativism and our sense of frustration. We need to feel good about ourselves again.

Let us remember what we have here. Let us remember what we are talking about: a land of limitless space, a tolerant people, a fair people and a decent people... It is time we woke up. It is time we shook ourselves out of this lethargy. I hope that this national debate encourages all of us, all Canadians, to stand up, to speak up strongly and loudly and clearly for Canada.

I support the motion and I will campaign for it.

Chapter 7

The Fight for Canada

John Turner was appointed Finance Minister in February 1972, in the aftermath of the "Nixon Shocks" and the official suspension of gold convertibility of the US dollar a year prior. The international exchange and monetary crisis which followed caused global shock and consternation. An angry American eagle, then enmeshed in an unpopular war abroad, and soon to experience the national humiliation of Watergate, stalked its trade partners, blaming them for its domestic and international misfortunes.

Canada's special relations with the US were terminated overnight. Turner took the helm during a time of enormous US pressure at the bargaining table with Canada. His challenge to persuade the US that it would be counterproductive to try to resolve its balance of payment problems on the backs of its closest allies.

He was advised by one of the finest deputy ministers ever to grace Ottawa—the inimitable Simon Reisman, who, as a prominent figure at the establishment of GATT and a champion of Canadian multilateralism knew better than most the enormous pressures our powerful southern neighbour could bring to bear at the negotiating table.

Turner and Reisman saw eye-to-eye on the issues of the day, particularly on the strategies to fend off trade harassment from the United States. Upon his deputy's retirement from the public service in 1975, the Minister of Finance singled out Reisman's loyalty in "supporting not only policy but also his minister in personal terms... no one has a more fertile mind... but above all he has been dedicated to the public interest."

Throughout his lengthy career in public life, Turner was personally and intellectually committed to a reasonable partnership with the United States. His hands-on study of American power began as soon as he entered parliament in 1962. In fact, Turner served as the lead government questioner in the Standing Committee of Foreign Affairs, examining the Columbia River treaty—a treaty which would stir Canadian apprehensions over the long reach of US power as none had before.

The lessons he learned were highlighted in a speech to the National Water Conference of the Chamber of Commerce of the United States in December 1965, in which he told Americans that continentalism was foreign to his vocabulary. He warned that Canada would not continue exporting surpluses without pledges of "guaranteed access" to American markets.

In an historic address to the Empire Club in 1971, Turner dismissed criticisms that the Canadian government was anti-American, arguing that insisting upon a national rather than a continental energy policy was to protect Canada's birthright. He added prophetically that he doubted Canadians would contemplate, with favour, free trade with the United States because the political consequences would be irreversible.

In a recent conversation, he reminisced on the period:

> The prime minister gave me full authority to negotiate on all the serious trade and monetary issues that confronted us in those days. And I am talking about the full agenda: the Auto Pact, the issue of foreign investment, trade remedy measures such as the Michelin affair, the energy crunch and so on. I knew we had to be on the right wave length at the highest levels because there had been a lot of communication hang-ups at the time. So every three or four months I would go down to Washington, play tennis with George Shultz (Secretary of the Treasury) and have dinner with the secretary and the president (Nixon) at the White House. We never left until we had thoroughly understood one another's point of view and we always brought a lot of goodwill to the table. The president was very well briefed on Canada and impressed me enormously with his intellect.

As a liberal, Turner was a believer in free trade in principle. As Minister of Finance and Chairman of the International Monetary Fund at this critical juncture in world economic history, he worked to shape the international institutions that would help lift and prevent barriers to international trade. But the tough negotiations he had had with our powerful neighbours south of the border gave him a deep understanding of the dangers of comprehensive trade agreements between Canada and the US that did not secure subsidy definitions or freedom from American trade harassment. He would bring that wealth of experience to the "fight of his life" a little over a decade later.

Elizabeth McIninch

A Canadian's View of North American Water Resources Development

FROM A SPEECH TO THE NATIONAL WATER CONFERENCE OF THE CHAMBER OF COMMERCE OF THE UNITED STATES
9 DECEMBER 1965 – WASHINGTON, D.C.

"North American Water Resources Development" is the subject I was asked to look at. I don't know who worded that title, but as I looked closely at those five words, I asked myself, what exactly does that mean? Am I to look at water resource development in North America, or am I to look at the development of Northern American water? No difference, you say. Perhaps not, but to our Canadian ears, there is a great difference. Water resource development in North America is a nice, safe topic, although a wide one—how Canada uses its water and what are our plans for the future; how the United States uses its water and what are its plans for the future. Mexico and Central America should be included too, if the survey is to be really complete. Nothing particularly controversial here.

But "North American water." That sounds suspiciously like the suggestion that the waters of North America should be considered a "continental water supply," and that is where we in Canada say: "Hold on a minute!" We say there is Canadian water, and there is American water (and there is Mexican water), but we do not like the new vocabulary which calls our water "continental water."

Why not? After all, Canada has more water than any other country in the world. That's true: we estimate that we do have more than one-quarter of the world's fresh, liquid, surface water. Surely then, you will say to me, Canadians have water to spare... I suppose, therefore, that it is a natural reaction for you, with your large, thirsty population and industry, to look at our unused water and make proposals such as we have heard increasingly in the past couple of years that our surplus could be used to relieve your drought.

But let's just examine those two assumptions—our surplus and your drought. We're not so sure we have a surplus. Right now, perhaps, but what of the future? We in Canada do not expect that our population will remain at 20 million, nor that our industrial activity will remain at the present level, nor that our underdeveloped land in the north and west will always be so. Before we export any of our water—our most precious resource—we want to be sure that it is surplus to our needs. We want to project our potential growth into the reasonably foreseeable future. This growth will depend on water. We don't want to export our water now only to find later that we have imported your problems. After all, would your nation have thought one hundred years ago with its clean, fresh streams then providing a seemingly inexhaustible supply of water, that the supply would ever run short and that you would someday be looking outside of your own country for additional supplies?

And that question raises perhaps another, more important, question. I hope I may be excused for asking it, as an outsider, but do you really need any more water? Are you actually suffering from a drought?...

And what about that arid West, or Southwest, where we read of demand for water approaching or exceeding supply? When demand exceeds supply, there is a shortage. But shortage is a relative thing. As you are well aware, the Southwest US has more water per person than the Northeast. Actually, I am told, the consumptive use of water per capita in the Colorado River basin is nearly 100 times as great as in the Hudson-Delaware basin. That is because irrigation—your nation's largest water use—consumes such huge quantities. Does this mean a shortage of water—or an excess of consumptive use? You will have to answer that question, but there is a strong suspicion that much irrigation water is ineffectively used...

I can see some of you are saying, "What right has this foreigner to tell us how we should use our water?" I know exactly how you feel: we in Canada have the same reaction when visitors from another country tell us how we should conduct our affairs. It's none of my business. True, as long as you're using your water. But, when you ask us for our water to help solve your problems, then I think our concern is justified, and, after all, you did ask me to look.

The point I am trying to make is that when you talk about drought you may be spawning a myth that you are running out of water. The problem may be not so much that you have too little water, but that you may not be husbanding or distributing the water you have. We in Canada are just as guilty. The issue may be as much the management of water, as a shortage of water. And while we are taking about water management, let's talk about what we do with the water we do have. It's not just water we want; it is clean water.

I think one of the greatest water problems facing both our countries is that of pollution. In every centre of population and industry the situation is the same. There may be plenty of water, but it may be useless water...

Before we talk about more water, then, let's clean the water we do have...

There have been many problems and solutions over the years, but probably the most recent, and perhaps the largest study performed by the International Joint Commission is now going on with respect to water levels and pollution in the Great Lakes, that magnificent water resource which we share.

In the fifty-odd years that the Commission has been operating it has provided a magnificent example (I would say unique) of international cooperation—an example to show the world that the settlement of boundary and trans-boundary water problems can be peacefully worked out between good neighbours.

There have, however, been suggestions recently that the Commission should extend its studies farther afield than the boundary. For example, one solution to the Great Lakes' low levels, put forward by some people (in both your country and ours) has been to divert some of Canada's northern rivers, now flowing into Hudson Bay, south into the Great Lakes. There was some pressure, in fact, to include such a study within the last reference to the I.J.C. on Great Lakes levels.

The Canadian government, quite reasonably I think, could not agree to this. Not that we object to the idea of studying the possibility of diverting our northern rivers; nor that we object to the idea of diverting these waters into the Great lakes. But we did not want to open a precedent of having a study of a strictly domestic resource made by an international board. We want, as Canadians, to look at these Canadian waters ourselves, to examine all possible uses, and come up, if we can, with the optimum use of these waters for Canada, wherever that use may be... (A) proposal which has received a great deal of publicity, perhaps because of its breathtaking magnitude and stupendous cost ($100 billion), is the so-called North American Water and Power Alliance (NAWAPA), conceived and proposed by a firm of consulting engineers in California. I am sure you have heard of it. It would store water in Canada—water from Alaska and Canada—and distribute it as far south as California and even Mexico, and east as far as the Great Lakes. I believe Senator Frank Moss of Utah has recently introduced a resolution into the US Senate concerning this project. The resolution would have your government ask Canada to refer jointly the NAWAPA project to the I.J.C. for study and recommendation.

As far as I am aware, Canada has not been asked officially by the United States government to give any comments regarding the project. What is the Canadian reaction? Cautious, I think would be the most descriptive expression. Cautious because 70 to 80 percent of the water in this project must come from Canadian rivers.

We are by no means sure that the best use of this water would be in California, or Mexico, or North Dakota, or Ohio. We may find a better use for it in British Columbia, Alberta, or Saskatchewan. We do not agree that continental development necessarily means the increasing concentration of population and industry in already existing centers. We feel that true continental development should include the development of Canadian population and industry, and its expansion into Canada's empty northland. I believe that any of you who may be from Idaho or Oregon will appreciate our reaction... Why not come a little further north where there is even more space, cleaner water, and purer air?

Now, I am not insisting that this will be our final reaction. It may be that, after we have studied all the alternatives, we would find that it would be to our advantage to sell some of our water, as we sell wheat, wood, and other resources. But we have to remember water is not quite the same. There is no substitute for water (although someday desalinization of sea water may give you alternative sources of supply). All economic development is limited by the amount of water available. Also, sales of other commodities cease when our own country requires these commodities. But can diversion of water be stopped once the die has been cast? Invest $100 billion in diversion and other works. Establish uses and industries based on the diversion. Can the diversion then be stopped as a wheat or an oil sale can be stopped? Not easily, I think you will agree.

This is why we feel it necessary to be cautious when discussing diversion of our water to another country. We want to be sure that our own needs will be met now and that our growth will be protected for the reasonable foreseeable future—before we consider any of our water to be surplus.

For this reason, Canada is not yet prepared to think in terms of a continental water policy, whereby we negotiate the sharing of the water of North America with the United States. Before Canada can contemplate export or sale of water to the US by way of diversion of our rivers or the creation of new water basins and canals, we must first achieve a better coordination among our own federal-provincial governments over the use of water. You may have the same problem of governmental coordination in the United States, although your *Water Resources Planning Act* is a great step forward. And we will have to agree in Canada (as you will in the US), among the various users and uses of water—to reconcile the priorities or balance the equities for water use.

We in Canada will also have to make a complete inventory, on a national scale, of our water resources, so that we know how much we have... Only when we are in possession of these facts will Canada be in a position to negotiate with the United States. And if someday we can agree to the sharing of this continent's water by offering some of our water for export, we might want at that time to insist that if water is to be considered as a continental resource, markets should also be considered on the same basis. We might wish to export water not for money (as we sold power under the Columbia River Treaty), but in return for access to your markets.

That, as I see it, must be our position. I don't want to sound tough. I hope I am merely being realistic. Americans have always appreciated realism and straight talking.

We in Canada recognize that the United States is our closest neighbour, and we consider you to be a very good neighbour. Our relations have always been friendly and we hope they will always remain so. We happen to share most of the North American continent—indeed we are co-tenants, as President Kennedy said to our Parliament in 1961. Our futures are, in this way, inextricably bound together. We are both fortunate in our natural resources, although not necessarily equally so in all resources. There is no reason why we should not continue to make use of these resources to our mutual and individual advantage.

Water will occupy the best minds of our two countries for the next generation. It will be a constant topic of discussion over our neighbourhood fence. I am sure that we will be able to resolve the future use of the water of this continent in a spirit of realistic friendship.

Plain Talk

FROM A SPEECH TO THE EMPIRE CLUB
18 NOVEMBER 1971 – TORONTO, ONTARIO

I do not believe that Canadians would contemplate with favour a free trade area or customs union with the United States. The political consequences would be irreversible and would dilute or even destroy any claim we had to our own sovereignty.

One of the persistent criticisms I hear from businessmen when I travel about the country is that government has created a climate of economic uncertainty... I am told that business needs certainty and predictability in order to project and plan investment... I understand the quest for stability...

The pace of change, the immediacy of communication, bigness, remoteness, and anonymity in government, have compelled new efforts to rectify the imbalance between the citizen and the state—new remedies, new avenues of appeal, new efforts to participate in the decision-making process... That is one reason I am here. To try to dissipate some of the breach in communication between your government and you, the business and professional community...

I have heard it said in recent weeks that the Canadian government is anti-American. That is not true. That it is being said is a reflection of a serious communication gap. I reject any attempt to quote certain remarks of the prime minister of this country completely out of context in order to build this case. Policy is not made nor interpreted by isolated or selected citation. Policy must be found from the deliberate words and acts of government.

Your government is not anti-American. If you were to ask me, anti-Americanism is bad politics in Canada. I believe there is too much community of interest, too many family ties, too much shared experience, to tolerate any permanent breach in our relationship with the US... Protection of our Arctic waters from pollution is not anti-American. We have a right to protect our environment and a duty to the world to cooperate in saving the seas from either oil or nuclear pollution.

Insisting upon a national rather than a continental energy policy is not anti-American. It is protection of our birthright. Resisting a continental resources policy is legitimate self-interest in any country that wants to find jobs for our people. A national water policy is not anti-American; it is a careful husbanding of our future. Resisting a landlord–tenant confrontation on this continent is inherent in our national self-respect.

If there has been any straining of our friendship with the United States, that surely has resulted from American initiatives. Two events have clouded our rapport with the Americans, one economic, one environmental: the imposition of the 10 percent surcharge on imports by President Nixon, and the nuclear test on Amchitka. These United States' actions, taken together with pending economic proposals before Congress, have provoked a wide range of emotion in Canada—from impatience to worry to bitterness...

On the matter of Amchika, the House of Commons passed a resolution calling for cancellation of the test... these are the facts and they lend no support to an anti-American posture. This is not to deny that the current situation will prompt some economic and political decisions of the first magnitude. In making them, Canadians will undoubtedly be forced to debate the essential continuing aspects of our association with the Americans... I believe, however, that a wise national policy should resist any action based on jingoistic or chauvinistic rhetoric, however emotionally satisfying that may be. Rather, a wise national policy would insist upon a balance, reconciling political sovereignty with economic stability...

There are limits, I think, to our present manoeuvrability in revising our economic position in North America. It is prudent to remind ourselves that no country is truly economically independent, not even the United States... Our economy, though healthy, is vulnerable in the sense that one-quarter of our gross national product depends on foreign trade and two-thirds of that trade is with a single customer, the United States... In the short term, we must devise our response to the current American surcharge and other ancillary economic measures currently before Congress—export subsidies and domestic investment tax incentives. We must diversify our trade... in the long term, we must gradually move towards a more independent control of our own business and resources, while ensuring that our actions do not unnecessarily jeopardize our economy nor impede the growth of our own manufacturing industries.

First the surcharge. The 10 percent imposition (which is, in fact, a disguised devaluation of the American dollar) affects between $2 billion and $3 billion of our sales. That alone is bad enough. What is worse is the uncertain duration of the surcharge... Underlying that uncertainty is a confusion about basic long-term objectives of the United States... Is this a deeper reflection of a new protectionism, a new isolationism?... We apply no unfair restrictions against US goods. We have one of the most open markets in the world...

We are now exploring the full range of fiscal, monetary, exchange, and tariff tools to meet any prolonged imposition of the American policy. The Americans at last are beginning to talk and to negotiate... In world trade, we need a new aggressive style of multilateral commodity trading. The ground rules have changed—perhaps for a long time, perhaps forever. The new protectionism of the United States and Britain's entry into the Common Market cloud our trading prospects... new trading blocs and abnormal currency values endanger our prosperity...

Surely we must explore our rights under the GATT treaty and attempt to revive a general movement towards freer trade... We need new economic tools... more important, we have to renew the dialogue between government, labour, and business... We cannot easily afford confrontations between the public and the private sector, between government and business, or between business and labour... Until our markets are assured and our unemployment dissipated, that type of confrontation spells self-inflicted economic punishment...

On the longer term, I favour a deliberate national policy, broadening and strengthening the Canadian economy. We need to seek means to lessen our economic vulnerability and to increase our scope for independent action and enhance our sense of national purpose. I do not believe that Canadians would contemplate with favour a free trade area or customs union with the United States. The political consequences would be irreversible and would dilute or even destroy any claim we had to our own sovereignty...

Any move towards more control over our own economy should be made, I believe, in positive, not negative nor retroactive terms... I do not believe that we should indiscriminately discourage foreign investment (apart from takeovers of existing firms), nor do I believe that we should or could "buy back" any investment already made... We have to seek rules under domestic and international law for multinational corporations...

Robert Frost used to say that "good fences make good neighbours." We are not quite sure whether the United States wants to raise the fence or tear it down. We are not sure whether they want to shut us out or take us over, or both... In our constant search for a national identity and independence, we have reacted defensively to the United States. The urgency of the moment provides us with the challenge now to strike out on a positive course that is pro-Canadian and anti-nobody.

FROM A SPEECH TO THE UNITED STATES COUNCIL OF THE INTERNATIONAL CHAMBER OF COMMERCE

10 DECEMBER 1973 – NEW YORK, NEW YORK

There was a time in years gone by when this kind of evening would have been devoted largely to extolling the image of happy handshakes across the world's longest undefended border. But as President Nixon suggested when he visited the Canadian Parliament in April of last year, nothing is to be gained by trying to gloss over the fact that more recently some very real problems have developed between us...

An open recognition of a problem is a first prerequisite for its solution. We do have differences. But the recognition of this fact should not be allowed to obscure another and more basic reality, one that still remains as true today as it was a dozen years ago when it was underlined by the late President John F. Kennedy in a similar address to the Canadian Parliament. "What unites us is far greater than what divides us," he said. "The issues and irritants that inevitably affect all neighbours are small indeed, in comparison with the issues we face together, above all, the sombre threat now posed to the whole neighbourhood of this continent and in fact to the community of nations..."

While the nature of the threat to which he alluded, that of communist aggression, may have diminished with the passage of the years, today we face another threat together of equal magnitude in scope... an energy shortage that jeopardizes the economy of the entire industrialized world... This energy crisis... is a common international problem. But it has been a cause of some friction between us, the latest of a series of elements that have contributed to the development of various stresses and strains in our relationship during the past two years...

Some upheavals have taken place in your country alone, but we have been caught in the fallout! There was Vietnam and its crisis of conscience, Watergate, and the sharp devaluation of the dollar to adjust to the radically altered balance of economic power in the world...

The actions begun by your government in August, 1971 to correct the dangerous imbalance in your international payments were necessary—and they were understood by Canadians to be necessary. What we did not understand was your failure to recognize that we had not contributed in any significant way to the underlying weakness in your balance of payments, as your government formerly had recognized in exempting Canada from previous balance of payments measures stretching back over a decade... We were nevertheless more vulnerable than any other nation to these measures of two years ago—such as the temporary tariff surcharges... simply because we are one another's best customers. Trade between our two countries in goods and services likely will amount to more than $40 billion this year, substantially more than between any other two nations on earth.

Basic differences of opinion between our two governments over the Canadian–United States balance of payments relationship led to controversy as well over such specific issues as the automotive pact and defence production sharing arrangements. Fortunately these controversies are beginning to fade into history as the trading position of your country improves...

At the same time, however, it is important to recognize that Canada itself is changing. And that fact compels both of us to re-assess our relationship. Canada has been described as a nation in search of an identity, but we are finally beginning to find it. In part, this is manifested by the growing determination of Canadians to play a more active role in shaping our own destiny. We want to be able to stand more squarely on our own feet, to increase our ownership and control of the resources of our own country, to work towards the greatest degree of economic and political independence that is possible in an increasingly interdependent world.

None of these developments should be construed as anti-American. On the contrary, they are very much in keeping with the new approach to foreign relationships by your government that has come to be termed the Nixon doctrine... Our determination to shape our own economic destiny is reflected in a broad framework of policies and programmes which have either been adopted within recent years or which are in the process of being formulated.

One illustration of this evolving framework is provided by the measure which I proposed in my first budget of May 1972, to reduce substantially the tax burden borne by manufacturing and processing industries, so as to strengthen their competitive position at home and abroad...

Now let me (discuss) the energy issue. To judge from some of the reports that have appeared in your press, you might understandably have the impression that we in Canada are a nation of ogres, miserly hoarding a vast underground ocean of oil in your hour of need and charging outrageous prices for what little we were prepared to ship across your borders. Nothing could be further from the truth. Let me outline the facts...

While I have no wish at this point to engage in recriminations, which cannot be helpful, I might point out that one of the important factors constraining the development of our reserves and productive capacity has been the restrictions which successive US governments have imposed on Canadian oil imports from 1959 until early this year. Because the massive escalation in the demand by your country for Canadian oil early this year threatened to create critical shortages in our own markets, we had no other practical alternative but to establish export controls in order to regulate the flow across the border...

Although our own supplies remain reasonably adequate to meet normal domestic requirements westward from Ontario, we are confronted by the danger of a shortage of petroleum supplies in Quebec and the Atlantic provinces because of the heavy reliance on imports to which I referred earlier. While President Nixon has estimated that the United States could face a nation-wide petroleum supply shortfall of some 17 percent, there is a possibility—if worse comes to worse—that eastern Canada could suffer a shortfall of some 20 percent.

Another source of misunderstanding with which I would like to deal is the export tax which we began to levy on petroleum shipments to your country, a tax that was initially set at 40 cents per barrel of crude oil and as of December amounted to $1.90 a barrel. The basic purpose of this tax was to help forestall an increase in prices charged to Canadian consumers by reinforcing the temporary price freeze voluntarily agreed to by the major integrated oil companies on their sales to Canada ... At the same time, however, we were also anxious to ensure that the return on Canadian oil sold in your market was not significantly less than that being received both for oil imports from other countries, or for the so-called "new oil" produced in your country that has been fully exempted from price controls...

While the threat posed to the whole industrialized world by the developing oil shortage should not be minimized, it is critically important also that it should not be exaggerated out of all proportion... To paraphrase President Roosevelt's warning 40 years ago, "we have nothing to fear but fear itself..."

To date we have no way of knowing what the shortfall will be and certainly the situation remains very volatile... (but) there is much that can be done by individuals and industries to conserve energy without affecting either unduly... While we must obviously continue to be prepared to take action to deal with problems as they arise, there is certainly no cause for panic... In my own view, the greatest threat does not come from an energy shortage as such, but from the danger of psyching our economies into a recession.

This energy crisis is only the most recent of a number of problems we have had to face as a result of many far-reaching changes going on around the world. These changes have caused stresses and strains between our two countries in recent years, but I believe these will ease as we go through the process of adjusting to a new, but still very special relationship.

Both of our countries are afflicted by the worldwide problem of inflation. Both share a common concern and a considerable similarity of interest over reform of the world's monetary system... Let me say this, as a friend, we need the world leadership of the US to solve these problems... I urge you to get back your confidence, avoid the temptations of isolationism and lead—fill the vacuum!

There is no denying that difficult problems confront all industrial nations. That makes it all the more important for us to stay cool, all the more important for us to remember the crucial lesson of the early '30s when self-serving actions by individual nations to isolate themselves from the rest of the world proved self-defeating for every nation. If we want to prevent history from repeating itself, with consequences that could be very far-reaching in the much more interdependent world that exists today, it is essential that all of the industrial nations maintain the closest consultation and cooperation. If we continue to stand together, there is no problem confronting us that we cannot eventually overcome together. And that is even more so the truth for the Canada–US relationship. We do over $40 billion of business a year. No two nations have more to gain and more to lose by not keeping in touch.

Chapter 8

The Free Trade Battle

John Turner's opposition to the Free Trade Agreement negotiated by Prime Minister Brian Mulroney and his government was clear and consistent when one considers Turner's thinking and hands-on experience in Canada–US relations back to the 1960s. A close friend of Robert Kennedy, and a man who later spoke at Richard Nixon's eightieth birthday party, he was no knee-jerk anti-American, like many (even in his own party) who took up the cause against FTA during the 1988 election.

As the election campaign began that Fall, in a move that has never fully been explained by the perpetrators, Turner's leadership came under attack. The seventieth prime minister stared down the internal dissenters and mounted his impressive attack on the FTA. Even his two external opponents that Fall, NDP Leader Ed Broadbent and Prime Minister Mulroney, later commented in books and during tributes in the Commons on Turner's bravery and skill on the stump in 1988.

With his intellectual groundings understood and clearly laid out, his "Crusade for Canada" regarding the FTA is logical. Turner was heading a party with only 40 MPs, a group that hadn't been out of power for any lengthy period of time since the days of John Diefenbaker. Ironically, Mulroney faced the same challenge later albeit with the positions reversed for his party. Bringing his party along with him in the lead-up to this historic national debate was anything but smooth. After the debates, Turner and Mulroney carried the fight on personally.

The business community lined up against Turner, although many senior leaders in this sector were his personal friends. Regardless, Turner put these strained relations aside and went forward with his opposition. His exchange with the prime minister in the English language FTA debate is now part of history. Turner, for a time, single-handedly galvanized public opinion and concerns about the FTA in English Canada that night. A new election dawned the next morning.

It is pointless today to argue over who "won" that election or who "lost." Elections Canada voter participation figures prove that all Canadians were victors in that election. More than 75 percent of eligible voters cast their ballots for or against Free Trade 20 years ago this Fall. Families debated the merits of the policy over dinner. Students were engaged on campuses. We debated in our workplaces as well. Canadian democracy has never since been as healthy as it was in 1988.

Again, Elections Canada figures speak for themselves. By 2004 for example, only 60.9 percent of eligible voters bothered to participate, a drop of about 15 percent. The more recent figures would be more dramatic.

Had Turner not stared down his internal foes, demonstrated his personal skill as a campaigner and debater, and brought his unique experience to the subject that year, Canadians would not have had the chance they had to fully participate in the most historic and crucial issue-based election of our time.

Arthur Milnes

FROM A SPEECH TO THE LIBERAL PARTY REFORM CONFERENCE
9 NOVEMBER 1985 – HALIFAX, NOVA SCOTIA

We Canadians are a unique and vibrant and diverse culture. We have some respect in the world as a voice of moderation and a voice of common sense. But we are going to have to preserve our dignity as a nation by speaking out loudly, boldly and proudly without hesitation.

It is within this context of course, that we as Liberals and as Canadians must examine the free trade proposal of our government. Because our prospective relationship with the United States, as advanced by the Conservative government in Ottawa, touches that very issue of sovereignty, it is going to be the most important political and economic decision of the next decade or so for Canada.

In this party we have always favoured enlarging our mutual access to our respective markets. We have always believed in enlarging our bilateral arrangement with the United States, usually however, within a multilateral context. We believe that it is a good idea to open discussions with the United States but we believe that the government of Canada is going about it the wrong way.

We believe, first of all, that before we enter formal negotiations, upon which we are now embarked, we should have had a full public debate in this country. We believe that the government of our country should have told us what is negotiable and what is not negotiable. What is on the table and what is not on the table? We should have received a cost benefit analysis. That is to say, what jobs are at risk, what jobs will be favoured, what industries are at risk, what industries will prosper, what regions will hurt, what regions will prosper?

Donald Macdonald (Chairman of the Royal Commission on the Economic Union and Development Prospects for Canada which recommended that Canada pursue free trade with the United States), who did us the honour of appearing at this conference, is a former colleague of mine and a man for whom I have the greatest respect. Donald told us that we had reached a stage in our history where Canada and Canadians should take a "leap of faith." I have said to Donald publicly and I have said to him personally: "Donald, you want us to take a leap of faith—that is too big a jump. Unless we know where we are going to land, that is too big a jump."

Not only has there been no more public debate, but a deliberate clandestine manipulative policy of keeping the debate under wraps. The provinces have not been intimately involved. The provinces have not been involved in any meaningful way at all...

I have the deepest conviction, after having travelled around this country, that while most Canadians want us to enlarge our trading relationship with Americans, and most Canadians enjoy the relationship we have with the United States, Canadians do not want to risk the independence of our country or our political sovereignty or economic manoeuvrability or our cultural identity or our identity as Canadians by any relationship that might involve trade with the United States. They don't want that. And we are going to be watching it very carefully.

On your behalf, members of our Caucus and I are going to be watching it particularly carefully. I would suspect, particularly here in Atlantic Canada, there must be several people in this room who some time in your lives had the opportunity of going down and working in the United States. Look at the exodus we have had from Atlantic Canada, and look at the exodus we have had from British Colombia. Yet every one of us is here and every one of us has stayed because we made a deliberate choice. We wanted to stay here. Why? Because we enjoy the British Parliamentary tradition. We enjoy the spirit of tolerance. We enjoy the style of federation we have. We enjoy the environment. We enjoy the outdoors, the frontier, the north. We enjoy the special community called Canada, and even though it costs us a little more money to remain as Canadians, the price of being Canadian is a price worth paying.

FROM A TELEVISED ADDRESS TO THE NATION ON THE FREE TRADE INITIATIVE IN RESPONSE TO THE PRIME MINISTER
16 JUNE 1986 – OTTAWA, ONTARIO

Tonight I want to tell you why we cannot support the Mulroney Trade Initiative with the United States.

Nothing could be more important than trade between Canada and our neighbour—or for that matter, Canada and the world—because we are a worldwide trader. Thirty cents of every dollar we earn comes to us from trade. Trade means jobs for all of us.

The Liberal party has always favoured widening trade—and lowering trade barriers—but on a worldwide basis. We feel that Canada has always done better in negotiations with the United States as part of international trade negotiations. The United States is our largest and most important trading partner, but it is not our only trading partner. Taking on a country ten times stronger than we are in an exclusive trade negotiation holds great risks for us, particularly when we believe that in the current negotiations, the preparation and the homework have not been done by our government.

Canadians do not know where Mr. Mulroney really stands. Sometimes he talks about free trade; then freer trade; then enhancing trade; and recently in Toronto, trade arrangements, industry by industry. We don't know where he stands, and the country does not know where he stands. Is free trade just another slogan like "sacred trust"? Has the prime minister really thought it through?

Negotiations with the Americans are off to a bad start. We think Mr. Mulroney has played our hand very badly. He has given away our cards too early. He has dismantled the Foreign Investment Review Agency. He has scrapped the National Energy Program. He has given away part of our book publishing industry, and all of this before negotiations even started. These were the very things that the Americans wanted most.

The homework hasn't been done. There has been no public debate in Canada—no public discussion. Free trade wasn't mentioned in the last election campaign. Mr. Mulroney has no mandate from the people of Canada to negotiate a comprehensive free trade arrangement.

Even more important, Canadians have not been given the facts. What is on the negotiating table? What isn't? Which industries are involved? Which industries are not on the table? Where are the new jobs? How many jobs will be lost? Because you know and I know that in every trade negotiation, there is give and take. There are winners and losers. And as Canadians, we have a right to know...

The timing of these negotiations couldn't be worse. The Americans face an election this November. Their Senators and their Congressmen are protecting American jobs—at our expense.

The Americans are looking at our $20 billion trade surplus and they are saying that they want to cut this number down to zero. And because of the way our government has handled itself, we are now in a trade war with the United States at the same time as we are supposed to be having negotiations. Have you asked yourselves, what happens if these negotiations now fail? Are we prepared for that contingency, because we will be worse off having put the spotlight of US protectionist forces so strongly on our own country.

One other thing: these trade negotiations are not a substitute for an active national economic policy, a policy which improves productivity and our ability to compete around the world. Our government seems to have abandoned this objective by placing all our eggs in one basket with the United States.

The whole thing has been botched right from the beginning. The prime minister is relying solely on his personal relationship with the president of the United States. We have already seen that that is not enough.

So, for all these reasons, we cannot and do not support the Mulroney initiative on trade.

As a matter of fact, we don't think there will be a comprehensive free trade arrangement because not even Mr. Mulroney wants to open up our auto pact with the United States. We don't believe Canadians want our agricultural support programs, nor do we want our broadcasting, our radio, our newspapers, our publishing companies—our cultural industries—subjected to free trade.

So we don't know what our government is really after, or what kind of agreement they have in mind. But I can assure you that we will follow these negotiations very closely.

And one thing is sure. We will not allow any agreement with the United States to limit our political independence as a nation. Our national sovereignty, our independence, our cultural identity, our regional economic equality—these are important to us. These are Canadian. We don't want them negotiated away.

We Canadians have built a unique community in North America. We like it here. We like our system of government, our spirit of tolerance, safety on our streets, our way of doing things. We do not intend to become the fifty-first State of the American Union.

Sure, it may cost more to live here. The price may be higher, but I believe that the price of being a Canadian is a price worth paying.

From a Speech to the House of Commons
18 December 1987 – Ottawa, Ontario

Mr. Speaker, this is more than a debate about trade. This debate is indeed about the kind of Canada we intend to leave to our children. Canadians have to make important choices if tomorrow's Canada is to be sovereign, independent, and dynamic. I believe that Canadians can make the right choices to control our own future without sacrificing our economic independence, and without submitting to the lure of continentalism.

We have the privilege of living in the freest, most tolerant country in the world. Our Charter of Rights, our social safety net, our unshakeable sense of fairness, are proof that we do have a deep commitment as a people to improving the quality of life of all of our citizens. This debate compels us, first, to think of Canada. I believe it appropriate and relevant for me to tell you, Mr. Speaker, what Canada means to me. It means our sense of tolerance, our unique history, our generous mix of cultures, our two official languages, our parliamentary system, our priceless environmental heritage, the cleanliness and safety of our big cities, and the special Canadian sense of fairness. It means when you go to a doctor or a hospital they do not ask to check your credit rating before they check your pulse.

Quite simply, and I am not ashamed to say it in this place, I love it here. I love what we have built as a nation, I love what we stand for, and above all, I love that it is ours. We have made a conscious choice to live here. We made a conscious choice to build this country against the odds, against the weather, against geography, and, against the unceasing pressures coming from south of our border. We made a conscious choice to build this country: east, west, and north. In order to bind it we built a railway, an airline, a broadcasting system, a pipeline, and a national highway. These are the links, the bonds we built against the raw force of continentalism which would have turned us south.

The trade deal would destroy those bonds by pulling us into a continental vortex dominated by the United States. What is worse, it will not be a conscious choice by Canadians because, if the Government has its way, Canadians will have absolutely nothing to say about it...

This country would never have been built east, west, and north without some resistance to those continental and economic forces. For 120 years we have resisted those forces and created a nation. Yet this agreement turns those forces north and south. Second, on the basis of pure economic forces and market forces, we would not have achieved some measure of economic equality in Canada. We would not have had a basis for our regional economic equality programs. We would not have had the basis for a philosophy that wherever one is born in the country, wherever one chooses to live when one comes to the country, or wherever one receives an education, one will have the same rights as a Canadian to a good education, a good job, and a secure retirement. Market forces would never alone have given us that. President Reagan has said that this deal represents the fulfilment of an American dream. I can understand that. Let the Americans dream, but we have our own dreams. We dream of an independent and distinct nation north of the 49th parallel.

From a Speech to the House of Commons on the Canada–United States Free Trade Agreement Implementation Act

30 August 1988 – Ottawa, Ontario

Mr. Speaker, the history of a country and a people is not written in one day. However, there are days in a country's history that are decisive for the future of its people, and the date of the next election is such a day. The prime minister is the only person who knows when that day will be, but when Canadians go to the polls, they will decide what happens to the Canadian–US Free Trade Agreement, the agreement that is the subject of our debate today. This debate concerns more than just our trade relations with our neighbours to the south, Canada's very future is at stake. The question is, what kind of country will we have at the beginning of the 21st century? Will Canada be independent, sovereign and autonomous, or will it be an American colony?

Canadians, better than any other nation, appreciate unity in diversity. That is why our country is officially and firmly bilingual and multicultural. Instead of homogenizing our citizens, our regions and our cultures, we cherish our differences because they make us unique, rich, proud, tolerant and responsible… We love this country. It is precious to us. Because we love this country, what we have built and what we stand for as Canadians, we will not allow it to be thrown away by the Government…

The Americans were born of revolution. We were born of the joining of British and French traditions. Their Constitution calls for life, liberty and the pursuit of happiness. The *British North America Act* called for peace, order and good government... For an American "you are either with us or against us." Choices are clear cut. We Canadians instinctively seek a consensus and a compromise...

We are more influenced by geography, by our environment, and by the vast expanses of wilderness reflected so dramatically in the paintings of Lawren Harris, A.Y. Jackson, and others of the Group of Seven. My favourite painter, Emily Carr, is from British Columbia. Every Canadian dreams, not only of his own home but of a cottage, a tent beside a lake or a river. With all the black flies, the mosquitoes, and the thunderstorms, it is his own escape, his retreat in the wilderness, something he can call his own. That is very much a part of us...

This agreement talks about the free flow of market forces. I believe in the market system, in competition, in private enterprise and in rewarding success. However, I have to remind the House and through you, Mr. Speaker, Canadians from coast to coast that, historically, Canada was not built on free market forces. This country became a nation in 1867. Negotiations began in 1864 because it wanted to resist the continental pressures of the United States. This country deliberately built itself east and west and then north to resist those continental forces. We built a railway which brought British Columbia into Confederation in 1871. We persuaded Prince Edward Island to join this Confederation in 1873 with a direct guarantee for communication and transport. The Terms of Union in 1949 persuaded Newfoundland to come in under the same guarantees.

We built a railway. We built a national highway. We established a national broadcasting system. We established and built a national pipeline and a national airline—all to build an infrastructure that would hold a relatively small population together in a massive land mass. We deliberately resisted the market forces of the United States.

Free market forces alone would not have given us public housing, or a public transportation network, or the best medical system in the world, the Canadian Wheat Board, or a very comprehensive support system for the weaker elements in Canadian society. What I am saying is not anti-American; it is pro-Canadian. The Americans have always been our closest friends and our closest allies, as well as our best trading partner... Our Canada has horizons which go far beyond those envisaged in the Conservative trade deal. There is a better way. We reject this deal because it turns us into little more than a colony of the United States and, on the international scene, into merely a junior partner.

From the Televised English Language Leaders' Debate
25 October 1988

Turner: The prime minister hasn't answered this really in five hours of debate. He hasn't answered why he changed his own personal mind against a bilateral agreement with the United States. The Americans can't believe their good luck. No wonder the Senate of the United States passed this deal in one day, no wonder the House of Representatives passed it in one day, no wonder President Reagan says that this is the fulfilment of the American dream.

We gave away our energy. We gave away our investment. We sold out our supply management and agriculture. And we have left hundreds of thousands of workers vulnerable because of the social programs involved, because of minimum wages that we will have to start to compare and harmonize, because of the fact that they are in vulnerable industries. And really, I think the time has come, after five hours of debate, for the prime minister to really answer those questions and tell us why he is where he is and why he did not pull out when he did not get what he thought he should have got.

Mulroney: I have answered, Mr. Turner, every conceivable question that has been put to me both in English and in French directly on national television, and I don't think I need any lessons from you, sir, about answering questions...

Turner: I think the Canadian people have a right to know why, when your primary objective was to get unfettered and secured access into the American market, we didn't get it. Why you didn't put clauses in to protect our social programs in this negotiation... Why did that not happen? Why also did we get a situation where we surrendered our entire energy policy to the United States, something they've been trying to achieve since 1956? Why did we abandon our farmers? Why did we open our capital markets so that a Canadian bank can be bought up and we don't have reciprocity in the American market at all? Why did you remove any ability to control the Canadian ownership of our business? These are questions that Canadians deserve to have an answer to and we have not had an opportunity in six hours to deal with them in the way that would make you come out of your shell.

Mulroney: Well, Mr. Turner, you're about two feet away from me, I've been with you for six hours, I've responded to everything that you had to say. I responded openly to all questions by Canada's most distinguished journalists in English and French. There has been a most vigorous, and I think probably unprecedented, exchange of views. And yet, notwithstanding that, simply because you have an idea that only you have a proper interpretation of a given agreement, it's difficult for anyone to persuade you for the opposite. And so you ought not to blame me or blame Mr. Broadbent for that or blame the journalists...

Turner: I happen to believe you have sold us out. I happen to believe that, once you—

Mulroney: Mr. Turner, just one second—

Turner: Once any region—

Mulroney: You do not have a monopoly on patriotism—

Turner: Once—

Mulroney:—and I resent your implication that only you are a Canadian. I want to tell you that I come from a Canadian family and I love Canada, and that is why I did it, to promote prosperity.

Turner: Once any country yields its economic levers—

Mulroney: Don't you impugn my motives or anyone else's—

Turner: Once a country yields its energy—

Mulroney: We have not done it.

Turner: Once a country yields its agriculture—

Mulroney: Wrong again.

Turner: Once a country yields itself to a subsidy war with the United States—

Mulroney: Wrong again.

Turner: On terms of definition then, the political ability of this country to remain as an independent nation, that is lost forever and that is the issue of this election, sir.

Mulroney: Mr. Turner, Mr. Turner. Let me tell you something, sir. This country is only about 120 years old, but my own father

55 years ago went himself as a labourer with hundreds of other Canadians and with their own hands, in northeastern Quebec, they built a little town, schools and churches, and they in their own way were nation-building. In the same way that the waves of immigrants from the Ukraine and Eastern Europe rolled back the prairies and in their own way, in their own time, they were nation-building because they loved Canada. I today, sir, as a Canadian, believe genuinely in what I am doing. I believe it is right for Canada. I believe that in my own modest way I am nation-building because I believe this benefits Canada and I love Canada.

Turner: I admire your father for what he did. My grandfather moved into British Columbia. My mother was a miner's daughter there. We are just as Canadian as you are, Mr. Mulroney, but I will tell you this. You mentioned 120 years of history. We built a country east and west and north. We built it on an infrastructure that deliberately resisted the continental pressure of the United States. For 120 years we've done that. With signature of a pen, you've reversed that, thrown us into the north-south influence of the United States and will reduce us, I am sure, to a colony of the United States because when the economic levers go, the political independence is sure to follow.

Mulroney: Mr. Turner, the document is cancellable on six months notice. Be serious. Be serious.

Turner: Cancellable? You are talking about our relationship with the United States—

Mulroney: A commercial document that is cancellable on six months notice.

Turner: Commercial document? That document relates to treaty. It relates to every facet of our lives. It's far more important to us than it is to the United States.

Mulroney: Mr. Turner.

Turner: Far more important.

Mulroney: Please be serious.

Turner: Well, I am serious and I've never been more serious in all my life.

From John Turner's speaking notes at the platform, Orillia Museum of Art and History, Sir John A. Macdonald birthday celebration

11 January 2001 – Orillia, Ontario

As for myself, my course is clear, Macdonald said. A British subject I was born, a British subject I will die. With my utmost effort, with my latest breath, will I oppose the veiled treason which attempts by sordid means and mercenary proffers to lure our people from their allegiance.

But if it should happen that we should be absorbed in the United States, the name of Canada would be literally forgotten; we should have the State of Ontario, the State of Quebec, the State of Nova Scotia and State of New Brunswick. Every one of the provinces would be a state, but where is the grand, the glorious name of Canada? All I can say is that not with me, or not by the action of my friends, or not by the action of the people of Canada, will such a disaster come upon us.

Chapter 9

John Turner in Winter: 1990 to Present Day

> *Whig-Standard*: What do you want the history books to say about the Right Honourable John Napier Turner?
>
> Turner: That he put something back into the country, that he believed in public service, he believed in Canada, he stood up for Canada, never ducked, met the issues head on.
>
> Question and answer, *Kingston Whig-Standard*, 23 June 2000

John Turner's last night in the full national spotlight took place on the evening of 21 June 1990. With the party he had led since 1984 gathered in convention before him, he gave one of the greatest speeches of his career.

It was at that moment and during that speech that Turner seamlessly transitioned to elder statesman.

Like most retiring leaders, he withdrew quietly, though he remained a Member of Parliament until 1993. As a former prime minister and leader, he had much to contribute, but kept, as the old saying goes, his powder dry. Like other ex-leaders in Canadian history such as Sir Robert Borden he made sure his voice would matter when he chose to employ it.

In early 1991, he took to his feet in the Commons to debate the first Persian Gulf War. Having sat at the cabinet table with Lester Pearson, Paul Martin Sr. and as someone who knew Louis St. Laurent personally—all men who had helped shape the United Nations in its infancy—he was dismayed when the Liberal party, under new leadership and seeking easy political gain at a time of world crisis, was prepared to defy a UN that Canada had help found.

With our country on the verge of war, it was Turner who truly represented his party's historic past and the voices no longer able to be heard. By speaking out, he kept faith with a grand national party's true responsibilities and its legacy on the world stage, even if the party leadership at the time would not.

While building an impressive law practice at Miller Thomson in Toronto, he continued to fight to protect Canada's natural beauty through the World Wildlife Fund, and to canoe those many Canadian rivers he knows better than most.

Despite his busy life in Toronto, it has been rare for Turner to turn down a speaking request to appear before a young audience, particularly at universities. His message hasn't changed; get involved. Make changes. Fight for what you believe in. Public life is the highest calling there is, outside of religious vocations. Parliament and parties need you. Canada needs you.

John Turner in winter? Hardly.

He always had the same answer when well-meaning friends tell him he has to write his memoirs for history's sake. "I'm not a kiss and tell guy," he'd say. In this, Turner was just like another former prime minister, another House of Commons man whose time in Sir John A. Macdonald's chair was brief. Another leader who didn't write memoirs; a man named Arthur Meighen. Luckily for all, the journalist M. Grattan O'Leary, helped convince Meighen to leave his speeches to history.

"Arthur Meighen's public life will be judged by posterity on its merits," O'Leary wrote in his 1949 Foreword to Meighen's *Unrevised and Unrepented*, a collection of speeches.

> I believe that judgment will be more favourable than that passed by his contemporaries; that history will be more kind to him than the times in which he lived. Be that as it may, here in these speeches we at any rate are permitted to see what manner of man he was, the things which he believed, the loyalties for which he fought, the principles which he loved... We may agree or disagree with what we read, but we can have the satisfaction of knowing that it is the man himself who speaks to us and not the hollow voice of some actor behind a mask—that here from a great man are the words with which his tongue and heart stirred and enriched our country.

At age 80, Turner, as O'Leary would surely agree, enriches Canada still.

Arthur Milnes

The Gulf War

FROM A SPEECH TO THE HOUSE OF COMMONS
16 JANUARY 1991 – OTTAWA, ONTARIO

The matter which has brought the House together today under an emergency session could not be at once more sombre or more momentous.

Our words here by themselves will not decide war and peace, yet we in this House should not in any way diminish the importance of what we say. Above all, we should not diminish the importance of where Canada stands in these very grave days.

Let us be clear from the outset. All of us in this House are united in our desire to see Saddam Hussein out of Kuwait. While we may have differing views as to how that should come about, we are all agreed on that objective.

I am glad that the government recalled Parliament. As parliamentarians we have important decisions to make, but each member, like each Canadian, has a moral problem. We are all convinced that war is frightening and we have always been in favour of peace. But at what price? We can say that collective security is at stake and that we must act quickly, but then we can also plead for more time to make the sanctions work. We all know that Iraq has rejected any diplomatic initiative, any compromise, any avenue for a potential settlement, whether it come from France, Jordan, Yemen, the United Nations... Egypt, Algeria, and so on.

I think that the members who spoke before me gave a good description of the horrors of war, but the basic question is this: What alternative is left if sanctions, diplomatic moves and threats fail before the intransigence of Saddam Hussein? As a nation we have always defended the principle of the sovereignty of our country. We have been, and still are, among the highly respected members of the United Nations, so how could we choose to ignore our commitments in this instance?

The matter which seizes us today transcends the merely personal, the merely partisan, and the seeking of political advantage. This Parliament and our country, Canada, are faced with a clear choice. We can continue to stand behind the United Nations and its resolutions for which we voted, and which told Iraq what it must do to avoid war.

We can remain an integral part of the most determined demonstration of collective political will ever marshalled by the United Nations to stand up against aggression. In my view it is the choice which all our history and the long tradition of Canada's support for the United Nations oblige us to make today.

To do otherwise would repudiate the votes we have unfailingly cast in support of the United Nations resolutions. It would also repudiate our commitment to internationalism and to the United Nations, the hallmarks of the Liberal party and Canada's foreign policy for decades.

At the very moment when the United Nations has moved itself to take a strong, unambiguous and collective stand against a brutal aggressor, Canada should not break solidarity with the nations that are standing united against Iraq.

To do so would give Saddam Hussein what he has been trying unsuccessfully to achieve by every desperate means these past months and weeks.

It has been said that Canada should not stand up to Hussein because this is a dispute about oil on the other side of the world, that it is not in Canada's interest to become embroiled.

Others have compared a war in the gulf to Vietnam, saying it would be an American war for American interest. It has also been argued that the Persian Gulf countries were the creation of occupying colonial powers and many of these nations are mere fiefdoms with capricious and arbitrary borders.

The most persuasive argument against the use of force is that sanctions should be given more time to work.

In my view all these reasons are in the end invalid. None of them justifies any weakening of the collective will now mustered to hold to the United Nations resolutions.

Yes, there is oil at stake in this dispute. If this aggression were allowed, Hussein would control nearly one-quarter of the world's supply of oil. The prospect of being in thrall to him for oil is particularly ominous. To the United States, to Canada, and to other wealthy countries with their own oil supplies, it is a little more costly and inconvenient; to Europe, a little more serious; to Japan, it is vital;

to the third world, it is disastrous. Those are the countries that would be least able to pay ransom prices that would be imposed.

The United Nations has not stood up to Hussein for the sake of oil. The stake is much higher.

What about the Vietnamese comparison? The critical difference between what happened in Vietnam and what may happen in the Gulf is that now the United States is not acting alone, though it is ready to bear by far the largest burden. The nations of the world have arrayed an unprecedented military alliance against Iraq under the auspices, through, and with the authority of the United Nations.

The United Nations, not the United States, set the January 15 deadline. Anyone who knows the United Nations and knows that institution, knows that it is very jealous in being master of its own destiny. Nobody pushes the United Nations around, not even the United States. No one nation, especially not the United States, is able to impose marching orders on that institution.

No, this is not an American adventure. It is a United Nations action in collective security, one of the greatest historic developments of our time, certainly in my lifetime, since the Second World War, one with enormous impact for the future.

The credibility of the United Nations is at stake. You do not have to know much about history to know that the League of Nations, after it failed to respond to Manchuria and failed to respond to Abyssinia, was finished. Its credibility was sapped, diluted, gone. This is one of those important moments in history.

I know there are those who want to limit Canada's role to peacekeeping. The fact is peace must be established first and unilateral aggression repulsed before peacekeeping can be effective.

The whole history and tradition and commitment of the party to which I have belonged for 35 years has been in support of the United Nations. Our people were there at the beginning, upholding the principle of collective security and supporting the resolutions and actions of the United Nations.

This is a crucial test for that international organization. This is a crucial test for the United Nations, and Canada must support it. This is a crucial test for collective security, and Canada must support it.

The failure of the United Nations to act upon its resolutions would lead eventually to instability, to non-credibility and perhaps to international anarchy.

Aggressors would have hope of profiting from their aggression. Saddam Hussein would sponsor other Husseins, aggressors who would use chemical warfare on both the enemy and even on their own people as Hussein has done, aggressors who would use nuclear weapons should, God forbid, they possess them.

As to how the Persian Gulf states came to be, that makes an interesting historical study. I believe that history is irrelevant today. What is relevant is that there is a sovereign country, or was a sovereign country, called Kuwait, which was brutally invaded by a neighbour for no other reason except that it was coveted.

Even if the case for sanctions could be made, and it is a strong case, the issue today is not sanctions. The issue today is whether the United Nations resolutions will be obeyed. It was the United Nations that decided the date. It was the United Nations that decided not to wait for sanctions, and it was the United Nations that imposed its own deadline.

The issue before us, before the House and before the world, is whose will is going to prevail: the ambitious will of Saddam Hussein who would hold, at the very least, the Arab world under his thumb, or the collective will of the world, expressed as uniquely as it can be expressed, within the forum of the United Nations with a rare singleness of purpose never in my lifetime seen by an international body.

If the alliance against Iraq were to fall into disarray from good intentions, from walking too many last miles, the impact upon the future of the United Nations would be devastating to the future efforts of collective security. The United Nations would be fatally exposed as the League of Nations was so ruthlessly, as being simply incapable of standing up to aggression, even to a brutal bully like Hussein.

Canada has had a proud role in the United Nations right from the beginning. This country has stood by the United Nations even when other countries, including the United States, lost faith in that organization.

It is no accident that we have relied as Canadians upon the fiat of international institutions, the International Monetary Fund, and as the Minister of Finance knows, the General Agreements on Tariffs and Trade, and I will leave that argument alone. But with the United Nations we have believed in internationalizing our institutions. We have never treated the United Nations as irrelevant. We have never treated it as merely a talking shop. As Canadians we may have lost some idealism but we never lost faith in the United Nations.

This issue is one on which I had to break silence. Since June I have remained quiet except for the odd lecture at a university. I felt the question before the House was paramount for us as elected representatives of the people of Canada for our country. I felt that each member must speak out as a Canadian, and more than that, as a citizen of the world, because the future of the world order is at stake, and stability and future peace.

I believe that this Parliament has a duty to support the United Nations resolutions as those texts are written, and therefore, the resolution before this House.

From a Speech to the Orillia Museum of Art and History's annual Sir John A. Macdonald birthday celebration
11 January 2001 – Orillia, Ontario

This day should be a special day for all Canadians. There are many who feel that this day should be a national holiday, for on January 11 in the year 1815, in Glasgow, Scotland, John Alexander Macdonald was born.

In few other countries would a national hero be so neglected. In comparing Macdonald to Washington it is probably safe to say that Sir John played a greater role in forging the Canadian nation-state than Washington did in determining the nature of his United States. In addition, Macdonald was the more interesting personality. The irony is that the interesting human aspects of Macdonald's personality have been allowed to obscure the true greatness of the man.

Britain will never forget her Cromwell and her Pitt, and her Disraeli. The hero whose name we add to our list of immortals, John Alexander Macdonald, had much of the force of a Cromwell, some of the compacting and concilliating tact of a Pitt, the sagacity of a Gladstone, and some of the shrewdness of a Disraeli. To read the biography of John Alexander Macdonald is, essentially, to read a "new world biography."

His was a great lifespan. His official life reached back to 1844; think of that. Lord Palmerston was still premier of England when Sir John was an active leader in Canada. When Louis Napoleon was still emperor of the French, when John Tyler was president of the United States, when Bismarck was an obscure country squire, when Lincoln was unheard of, and when Theodore Roosevelt was yet unborn, Sir John A. Macdonald was well into his life task.

But our wonder grows when we reflect that that career was continued through 47 years of parliamentary life. He was the leader of his party for 36 years; he was a minister of the Crown for 35 years; he was premier of this Dominion for over 20 years. The public life of the average American statesman is very short: Lincoln was before the public but nine years, McKinley was in national prominence but 13 years, Cleveland, 15 years; Sir John A. Macdonald, 47 years. In those early days he did Canada great service.

I thought I'd place a quote on the record from Sir Wilfrid Laurier's speech in Parliament upon the death of Macdonald:

> The place of Sir John A. Macdonald in this country was so large and so absorbing that it is almost impossible to conceive that the politics of this country—the fate of this country—will continue without him. His loss overwhelms us. For my part, I say, with all truth, his loss overwhelms me, and that it also overwhelms this Parliament, as if indeed one of the institutions of the land had given way. Sir John A. Macdonald now belongs to the ages, and it can be said with certainty that the career which has just been closed is one of the most remarkable careers of this century...
>
> As to his statesmanship, it is written in the history of Canada. It may be said without any exaggeration whatever, that the life of Sir John Macdonald, from the time he entered Parliament, is the history of Canada. (Laurier, the House of Commons, 8 June 1891.)

Remember Macdonald's famous unity quote: "Let us be English or let us be French... and above all let us be Canadians."

D'Arcy McGee is an example of the patriotic feeling of the men from all the provinces Sir John A. brought together. Here is McGee on Canada: "I see in the not remote future one great nationality, bound, like the shield of Achilles, by the blue rim of ocean."

Patriotism: "Canada First... The Country Above Party," motto of Sir John's party, 1868 to 1875.

Throughout the 1860s, Macdonald worked in support of the confederation movement. There had been for several years a movement to unite the Maritime provinces. When the Province of Canada showed interest in confederation, a conference was held in Charlottetown on 1 September 1864. Each province was contending with its own anti-confederation forces, and Newfoundland would reject union outright. The more prosperous Maritime provinces felt confederation would weaken their autonomy. In Canada East (Quebec), there was fear that confederation would dilute French Canadian interests.

Finally, external events hastened the acceptance of confederation. The American Civil War, the Fenian Raids of 1866, and a generally aggressive American foreign policy caused concern about the defence of the British North American colonies.

Macdonald played a leading role in promoting confederation, to the point of making alliance with his staunch political rival and Opposition leader, George Brown. With his wide-ranging personal vision and constitutional expertise, Macdonald drafted the *British North America Act*, which defined the federal system by which the five provinces were united on 1 July 1867.

Macdonald was appointed prime minister of Canada and won the federal election the following month. In his first administration, his primary purpose was to build a nation. Communications between the provinces were essential and to this end, Macdonald began the national railway. It would run from Halifax to the Pacific coast and include Canada's two new provinces of Manitoba and British Columbia, and the Northwest Territories.

Under Macdonald's leadership, Canada achieved a certain degree of autonomy from Britain in foreign affairs. He also brought in a system of tariffs to protect Canadian products from foreign imports, especially those from the United States, in order to boost economic growth.

We as Canadians should remember him for his accomplishments. He was the leading Father of Confederation. As Canada's first prime minister, he was responsible for securing the West, in the face of a very real American threat. He saw the Canadian Pacific Railway through to its completion, against considerable opposition, and thus he created of Canada something more than a mere geographic expression. His national policy provided a framework within which a national economy would develop.

In the final analysis, he not only did more than anyone else to bring Canada into being, but he also ensured her survival through the early, difficult years. In doing so he earned, or should have earned, the title "Father of Our Nation."

"There is no paramount race in this country, we are all Canadians, and those who are not English are nonetheless British subjects on that account," he said.

An 1860 speech summed up his lifelong political creed and political goals: "One people, great in territory, great in resources, great in enterprise, great in credit, great in capital."

According to W. Stewart Wallace's *Macdonald* in the Canadian Statesmen series, Sir John A. once had a very interesting conversation with Principal Grant at Queen's University. "He once asked Principal Grant... why he no longer supported him," Wallace writes. "Principal Grant replied that he had always supported him when he thought he was right. 'Ah.' Sir John, sadly said. 'I have very little use for that kind of support.'"

He was great as a political leader; he was known as the Old Chieftain. He was born a leader; he had the peculiar quality which we call magnetism, which I suppose is another word for love. Magnetism is that quality which compels a man to walk 10 blocks out of his way in order to meet you, instead of walking 10 blocks out of his way in order to avoid you. Magnetism was the quality which Sir John held. A country Member of Parliament—I think his name was David Thompson of Haldimand—said:

> I was sick nearly all the session, and at the last I went back to Ottawa. The first man I met was Blake; he passed me with a simple nod as if he had forgotten I was away. Then I met Cartwright, who was just as cold. Then I met Sir John, who rushed across the chamber, slapped me on the shoulder, grasped my hand, and said, 'Davy, I am glad you are back again; I hope you will live many a day to vote against me.' It was pretty hard not to follow a man like that.

He had a prodigious memory; he could recall names and faces after a lapse of 30 or 40 years. In Vancouver in 1886 a man came up and said, "Sir John, you don't remember me."

"Oh yes," said Sir John, "in the picnic in 1856 out yonder in Lindsay you held an umbrella over me on a rainy day while I made a speech." And he recalled the man's name. He compacted his friends into a unit.

I suppose he would not be regarded as an orator quite of the class of Bryan or Laurier. I think he had several men in his party during his last years who were more finished orators than he would claim to be. And yet, if holding and arousing and convincing and persuading people is oratory, he was an orator.

When an MP disagreed with him in the House, Sir John A. said, "I have not the slightest objection to the Honourable Member retaining his opinion—if he will only give us his vote."

While Macdonald's administration accomplished great things, it also was fraught with difficulties. Revelations of the shady dealings between the Conservatives and the railway syndicate led to the Pacific Scandal in 1873. Macdonald's government was forced to resign and lost the election in 1874.

> We have faithfully done our duty," he said... "I have fought the battle of Confederation, the battle of the union, the battle of the Dominion of Canada. I throw myself upon this House; I throw myself upon this country; I throw myself upon posterity; and I believe, and I know that notwithstanding the many failings in my life, I shall have the voice of this country... rallying around me. And, if I am mistaken in that, I can confidently appeal to a higher court—to the court of my own conscience, and to the court of posterity. I leave it to this House with every confidence. I am equal to either fortune. I can see past the decision of this House, either for me or against me, I know—and it is no vain boast for me to say so... that there does not exist in this country a man who has given more of his time, more of his heart, more of his wealth, more of his intellect and power, such as may be, for the good of this Dominion of Canada.

He regained power in 1878, but political troubles continued. Macdonald's handling of the Northwest Rebellion in 1885 and the execution of Louis Riel outraged French Canadians, sparking an antagonism between them and English Canadians that would continue for years. The federal powers envisioned by Macdonald were weakened by legal challenges launched by the provinces...

He was also a man of humour. Recovering from a critical illness in 1870, Sir John A. was allowed half an oyster at dinner. Although he begged for more, the doctor refused, saying, "Remember Sir John, the hopes of Canada depend on you."

"Strange," replied the prime minister of Canada, "that the hopes of Canada should depend on half an oyster."

Told he had to rebuke McGee, he took D'Arcy aside one morning and said, "My boy, this is a small government we have, you know, here in Canada, and they think it is hardly large enough for two drunkards, and I guess you will have to quit."

There is also a variation on the Principal Grant quote I cited. It seems Sir John is told by a senator that the man remains a Tory and will always support Sir John A. when Macdonald is right. The great man replied, "That is no satisfaction. Anybody may support me when I am right. What I want is a man who will support me when I am wrong."

"I know enough to know that you would rather have Sir John A. drunk than George Brown sober," he once said.

> Gentlemen, I feel great pride in occupying the position that has been awarded me by the people of this country. I can, at my age, have no other wish than to live well in the minds of my fellow countrymen, and when I die, to live well in their recollection. [Cheers] I have had a long life of politics, a long life of official duties. I have tried, according to the best of my judgment, to do what I could for the well-being of good government and the future prosperity of this, my beloved country.

The right honourable gentleman resumed his seat amid loud and long-continued cheering.

I believe we can learn from Macdonald today.

I still think he was our greatest prime minister. He was a rousing stump speaker; he was riveting in Parliament. He understood, as few people have, the relationship between our two founding peoples. He reached out to Lower Canada, now Quebec, and he made it happen. He also understood our need to remain independent beside the then-overwhelming military power of the United States—now the military, economic and political power of the United States—and he launched his National Policy.

In other words, he understood the fabric of the country and our need to remain sovereign and independent from the United States.

Do we do enough to remember him?

No we don't. How about Washington's birthday in the United States? How about Lincoln's birthday? Do you know what I mean? How about the Jefferson Memorial, the Washington Monument?

January 11 won't do it (it's too close to New Year's and Christmas). How about the date of his death in 1891—June 6?

We need more heroes in Canada. Let's begin again with Sir John A.

Canada: a Vanishing Identity
From a Speech at St. Francis Xavier University
3 April 2002 – Antigonish, Nova Scotia

Coming down here we were remembering the great province here of Nova Scotia—how beautiful it is. And, of course, we're close to Mulgrave where my grandmother was born. And to Stellerton where my grandfather was the hoist engineer at the old mine before he campaigned for Sir Charles Tupper in 1896. Tupper lost and Wilfrid Laurier came in and the owner of the mine was a Grit, so my grandfather ended up in British Columbia, which is why our family grew up there. But in any event, I just thought that it is our good fortune as Canadians to live in this country, and let us remember it from time to time. I say this particularly to our younger people here tonight, that we occupy the most beautiful land on the face of the earth. It is our good sense that's made this country one of the most free and open democracies in the world...

If we, as Canadians, are to meet (our) national challenge in the global and continental world, we need to call on the best and brightest of the next generation to take an active role in the political life of this country. This is why I am glad to be here, President (Sean) Riley (of St. F.X.), before your students and alumni. We need more young people who are willing to set aside their own personal goals for a time and put the country first. That's what Allan J. MacEachen did. That's what Joyce Fairbairn did. That's what John Stewart did. I believe that's what I tried to do. We need more Allan J. MacEachens in the House of Commons. The best and the brightest.

When I was growing up and entering politics... I briefly got to know Jack and Bobby Kennedy... What Bobby Kennedy said to the young people of the United States (in the 1968 race for the Democratic nomination) applies to us right now. We need a new revival of participation in our public process. People who are willing to sacrifice something—family time, money, opportunities, privacy, for the public life of our country. You're part of the system too, and we can't take this public process for granted. We can't always leave it to someone else. We've got a great country. It's worth preserving. The challenges are immense and it won't happen unless more of you care and do something about it.

My dream, and I'm sure it's Allan J.'s dream, has always been that one day we would live up to our potential as a country. We never have quite lived up to our potential as a country. That was Sir Wilfrid Laurier's dream. It was also Sir John A.'s dream. And they still remain our greatest prime ministers. We've got such a great heritage and a great opportunity with our limitless land, our water, our resources, and our northern frontier. There's space to be alone when we want to; our two languages, our many cultures, our spirit of freedom and tolerance, our respect for the law, our faith still in parliamentary democracy. I think we all in this room want this nation to endure because millions of Canadians, I know, share my dream for our country—for a Canada that is strong and sovereign and united.

FROM A SPEECH TO THE UKRAINIAN CANADIAN CONGRESS
25 AUGUST 2005 – WINNIPEG, MANITOBA

At the request of Prime Minister Paul Martin, I missed my first Canadian Christmas in more than 50 years to lead Ottawa's election observation mission to Ukraine, after consulting with my wife and children before accepting.

Attending a Christmas mass in English in Kyiv was almost as if I had been in Toronto. The choir was great. And the priest was an Irishman, Father Paul Roche. It was an honour to be in Ukraine along with the other Canadians who sacrificed their Christmas because they felt that their presence would help ensure that democracy took hold in Ukraine.

This was a classic example of democracy trying to breathe. No foreign election has ever got this kind of attention in Canada. This was a crusade for democracy. The key to any democracy is a free and honest election. We were in Ukraine as observers, but observers only. We were impartial. We were prepared to accept a free, honest result. And when we were in Ukraine we all remained impartial and neutral.

The official Canadian delegation included almost 400 people Ottawa selected to work as part of an independent observer mission in the eastern European country. More than 100 others were part of a mission sponsored by the Organization for Security and Cooperation in Europe, an international group specializing in regional conflicts.

Our role was to provide an impartial assessment of whether the election in Ukraine was conducted in accordance with democratic standards. The observers were selected for their expertise in electoral work, knowledge of Ukraine and their perceived ability to handle the conflict that could plague the vote.

The mission represented the inaugural project for the Canada Corps, an initiative by the Canadian International Development Agency, aimed at sending Canadian experts where aid is needed abroad. The official observer team, the largest that Canada had ever fielded for any election, was hastily recruited and selected from more than 4,000 applicants—many of them first-time election monitors. They received two days of training in Ottawa and one day of Ukraine orientation in Kyiv before being deployed in 20 groups of 20 around the country. Each team had two monitors, at least one of whom spoke Ukrainian or Russian, and were sent to 10 to 12 polling stations.

The observers were accompanied by a driver and a translator, but they also benefited from additional staff Ottawa sent to its embassy in Ukraine to handle any unexpected crises. They actually had consular help right in the regions where they were deployed.

The delegation acted similar to scrutineers in Canadian elections, observing the voting process and monitoring polling stations to ensure free access.

The independent mission is to file a report on its observations within two months. The work of the Canadians for the OSCE mission did not overlap the independent mission's objectives.

The Ukrainian Canadian Congress was among several other Canadian groups sending 500 election observers to Ukraine, among the 8,300 monitors from around the world. The mission to Ukraine was ten times larger than any previous deployment of Canadian election monitors. The assignment was notable because no other foreign election had received so much international scrutiny.

Free, open and honest. That was the kind of election I hoped for in the Ukrainian election of December 26th. Advice to our people: it's Ukraine's election, not ours—be impartial, neutral, silent.

We were well received across the country. Canadian monitors found only minor violations of proper electoral procedure. Some (of the infractions) were technical, some were weaknesses of human error. None were deliberate. A good many were of a kind you could find in a Canadian constituency in an election. Among the problems noted by Canadian observers in a few polling stations were the presence of police near voting booths, refusal to admit international observers, voting without proper identification, improperly sealed ballot boxes and incomplete voter lists.

Canada was the first nation to recognize Ukraine as an independent country as the Soviet Union folded in 1991, and there are more than a million Canadians who claim to be entirely or partially of Ukrainian descent.

I was proud (and always will be), to be part of reinforcing this friendship in an impartial, prudent way.

About the Editors

Elizabeth McIninch is an international business consultant and editor of the Friendship Beyond Borders series that specializes in Canada's bilateral relations with selected countries abroad. A former Canadian history and government professor at John Abbott College in Montreal, she has been an archival assistant to the Rt. Hon. John Napier Turner since 1989.

Arthur Milnes is a journalist and Fellow of the Queen's University Centre for the Study of Democracy. He served as research assistant to the Rt. Hon. Brian Mulroney on the latter's Memoirs.

About the Editors

Elizabeth McIninch is an international business consultant and editor of the Friendship Beyond Borders series that specializes in Canada's bilateral relations with selected countries abroad. A former Canadian history and government professor at John Abbott College in Montreal, she has been an archival assistant to the Rt. Hon. John Napier Turner since 1989.

Arthur Milnes is a journalist and Fellow of the Queen's University Centre for the Study of Democracy. He served as research assistant to the Rt. Hon. Brian Mulroney on the latter's Memoirs.

Queen's Policy Studies
Recent Publications

The Queen's Policy Studies Series is dedicated to the exploration of major public policy issues that confront governments and society in Canada and other nations.

Our books are available from good bookstores everywhere, including the Queen's University bookstore (http://www.campusbookstore.com/). McGill-Queen's University Press is the exclusive world representative and distributor of books in the series. A full catalogue and ordering information may be found on their web site (http://mqup.mcgill.ca/).

School of Policy Studies

The Afghanistan Challenge: Hard Realities and Strategic Choices, Hans-Georg Ehrhart and Charles Pentland (eds.), 2009. Paper 978-1-55339-241-5

Measuring What Matters in Peace Operations and Crisis Management, Sarah Jane Meharg, 2009. Paper 978-1-55339-228-6 Cloth ISBN 978-1-55339-229-3

International Migration and the Governance of Religious Diversity, Paul Bramadat and Matthias Koenig (eds.), 2009. Paper 978-1-55339-266-8 Cloth ISBN 978-1-55339-267-5

Who Goes? Who Stays? What Matters? Accessing and Persisting in Post-Secondary Education in Canada, Ross Finnie, Richard E. Mueller, Arthur Sweetman, and Alex Usher (eds.), 2008. Paper 978-1-55339-221-7 Cloth ISBN 978-1-55339-222-4

Economic Transitions with Chinese Characteristics: Thirty Years of Reform and Opening Up, Arthur Sweetman and Jun Zhang (eds.), 2009
Paper 978-1-55339-225-5 Cloth ISBN 978-1-55339-226-2

Economic Transitions with Chinese Characteristics: Social Change During Thirty Years of Reform, Arthur Sweetman and Jun Zhang (eds.), 2009
Paper 978-1-55339-234-7 Cloth ISBN 978-1-55339-235-4

Dear Gladys: Letters from Over There, Gladys Osmond (Gilbert Penney ed.), 2009 Paper ISBN 978-1-55339-223-1

Immigration and Integration in Canada in the Twenty-first Century, John Biles, Meyer Burstein, and James Frideres (eds.), 2008
Paper ISBN 978-1-55339-216-3 Cloth ISBN 978-1-55339-217-0

Robert Stanfield's Canada, Richard Clippingdale, 2008   ISBN 978-1-55339-218-7

Exploring Social Insurance: Can a Dose of Europe Cure Canadian Health Care Finance? Colleen Flood, Mark Stabile, and Carolyn Tuohy (eds.), 2008
Paper ISBN 978-1-55339-136-4 Cloth ISBN 978-1-55339-213-2

Canada in NORAD, 1957–2007: A History, Joseph T. Jockel, 2007
Paper ISBN 978-1-55339-134-0 Cloth ISBN 978-1-55339-135-7

Canadian Public-Sector Financial Management, Andrew Graham, 2007
Paper ISBN 978-1-55339-120-3 Cloth ISBN 978-1-55339-121-0

Emerging Approaches to Chronic Disease Management in Primary Health Care,
John Dorland and Mary Ann McColl (eds.), 2007
Paper ISBN 978-1-55339-130-2   Cloth ISBN 978-1-55339-131-9

Fulfilling Potential, Creating Success: Perspectives on Human Capital Development,
Garnett Picot, Ron Saunders and Arthur Sweetman (eds.), 2007
Paper ISBN 978-1-55339-127-2   Cloth ISBN 978-1-55339-128-9

Reinventing Canadian Defence Procurement: A View from the Inside, Alan S. Williams, 2006 Paper ISBN 0-9781693-0-1 (Published in association with Breakout Educational Network)

SARS in Context: Memory, History, Policy, Jacalyn Duffin and Arthur Sweetman (eds.), 2006 Paper ISBN 978-0-7735-3194-9   Cloth ISBN 978-0-7735-3193-2
(Published in association with McGill-Queen's University Press)

Dreamland: How Canada's Pretend Foreign Policy has Undermined Sovereignty, Roy Rempel, 2006 Paper ISBN 1-55339-118-7   Cloth ISBN 1-55339-119-5
(Published in association with Breakout Educational Network)

Canadian and Mexican Security in the New North America: Challenges and Prospects,
Jordi Díez (ed.), 2006
Paper ISBN 978-1-55339-123-4   Cloth ISBN 978-1-55339-122-7

Global Networks and Local Linkages: The Paradox of Cluster Development in an Open Economy, David A. Wolfe and Matthew Lucas (eds.), 2005
Paper ISBN 1-55339-047-4 Cloth ISBN 1-55339-048-2

Choice of Force: Special Operations for Canada, David Last and Bernd Horn (eds.), 2005 Paper ISBN 1-55339-044-X Cloth ISBN 1-55339-045-8

Force of Choice: Perspectives on Special Operations, Bernd Horn, J. Paul de B. Taillon, and David Last (eds.), 2004   Paper ISBN 1-55339-042-3   Cloth 1-55339-043-1

New Missions, Old Problems, Douglas L. Bland, David Last, Franklin Pinch, and Alan Okros (eds.), 2004   Paper ISBN 1-55339-034-2   Cloth 1-55339-035-0

The North American Democratic Peace: Absence of War and Security Institution-Building in Canada-US Relations, 1867-1958, Stéphane Roussel, 2004
Paper ISBN 0-88911-937-6   Cloth 0-88911-932-2

Implementing Primary Care Reform: Barriers and Facilitators, Ruth Wilson, S.E.D. Shortt and John Dorland (eds.), 2004
Paper ISBN 1-55339-040-7   Cloth 1-55339-041-5

Social and Cultural Change, David Last, Franklin Pinch, Douglas L. Bland, and Alan Okros (eds.), 2004   Paper ISBN 1-55339-032-6   Cloth 1-55339-033-4

Clusters in a Cold Climate: Innovation Dynamics in a Diverse Economy, David A. Wolfe and Matthew Lucas (eds.), 2004
Paper ISBN 1-55339-038-5   Cloth 1-55339-039-3

Canada Without Armed Forces? Douglas L. Bland (ed.), 2004
Paper ISBN 1-55339-036-9   Cloth 1-55339-037-7

Campaigns for International Security: Canada's Defence Policy at the Turn of the Century, Douglas L. Bland and Sean M. Maloney, 2004
Paper ISBN 0-88911-962-7   Cloth 0-88911-964-3

Understanding Innovation in Canadian Industry, Fred Gault (ed.), 2003
Paper ISBN 1-55339-030-X   Cloth 1-55339-031-8

Delicate Dances: Public Policy and the Nonprofit Sector, Kathy L. Brock (ed.), 2003
Paper ISBN 0-88911-953-8   Cloth 0-88911-955-4

Beyond the National Divide: Regional Dimensions of Industrial Relations, Mark Thompson, Joseph B. Rose and Anthony E. Smith (eds.), 2003
Paper ISBN 0-88911-963-5   Cloth 0-88911-965-1

The Nonprofit Sector in Interesting Times: Case Studies in a Changing Sector, Kathy L. Brock and Keith G. Banting (eds.), 2003
Paper ISBN 0-88911-941-4   Cloth 0-88911-943-0

Clusters Old and New: The Transition to a Knowledge Economy in Canada's Regions, David A. Wolfe (ed.), 2003   Paper ISBN 0-88911-959-7   Cloth 0-88911-961-9

The e-Connected World: Risks and Opportunities, Stephen Coleman (ed.), 2003
Paper ISBN 0-88911-945-7   Cloth 0-88911-947-3

Knowledge Clusters and Regional Innovation: Economic Development in Canada, J. Adam Holbrook and David A. Wolfe (eds.), 2002
Paper ISBN 0-88911-919-8   Cloth 0-88911-917-1

Lessons of Everyday Law/Le droit du quotidien, Roderick Alexander Macdonald, 2002
Paper ISBN 0-88911-915-5   Cloth 0-88911-913-9

Improving Connections Between Governments and Nonprofit and Voluntary Organizations: Public Policy and the Third Sector, Kathy L. Brock (ed.), 2002
Paper ISBN 0-88911-899-X   Cloth 0-88911-907-4

Centre for the Study of Democracy

The Authentic Voice of Canada: R.B. Bennett's Speeches in the House of Lords, 1941–1947, Christopher McCreery and Arthur Milnes (eds.), 2009. Paper 978-1-55339-275-0 Cloth ISBN 978-1-55339-276-7

Age of the Offered Hand: The Cross-Border Partnership Between President George H.W. Bush and Prime Minister Brian Mulroney, A Documentary History, James McGrath and Arthur Milnes (eds.), 2009
Paper ISBN 978-1-55339-232-3 Cloth ISBN 978-1-55339-233-0

In Roosevelt's Bright Shadow: Presidential Addresses About Canada from Taft to Obama in Honour of FDR's 1938 Speech at Queen's University, Arthur Milnes (ed.), 2009
Paper ISBN 978-1-55339-230-9 Cloth ISBN 978-1-55339-231-6

Politics of Purpose, 40th Anniversary Edition, The Right Honourable John N. Turner 17th Prime Minister of Canada, Elizabeth McIninch and Arthur Milnes (eds.), 2009   Paper ISBN 978-1-55339-227-9 Cloth ISBN 978-1-55339-224-8

Bridging the Divide: Religious Dialogue and Universal Ethics, Papers for The InterAction Council, Thomas S. Axworthy (ed.), 2008
Paper ISBN 978-1-55339-219-4 Cloth ISBN 978-1-55339-220-0

Institute of Intergovernmental Relations

The Democratic Dilemma: Reforming the Canadian Senate, Jennifer Smith (ed.), 2009.
Paper 978-1-55339-190-6

Canada: The State of the Federation 2006/07: Transitions – Fiscal and Political Federalism in an Era of Change, vol. 20, John R. Allan, Thomas J. Courchene, and Christian Leuprecht (eds.), 2009
Paper ISBN 978-1-55339-189-0 Cloth ISBN 978-1-55339-191-3

Comparing Federal Systems, Third Edition, Ronald L. Watts, 2008
Paper ISBN 978-1-55339-188-3

Canada: The State of the Federation 2005: Quebec and Canada in the New Century – New Dynamics, New Opportunities, vol. 19, Michael Murphy (ed.), 2007
Paper ISBN 978-1-55339-018-3 Cloth ISBN 978-1-55339-017-6

Spheres of Governance: Comparative Studies of Cities in Multilevel Governance Systems, Harvey Lazar and Christian Leuprecht (eds.), 2007
Paper ISBN 978-1-55339-019-0 Cloth ISBN 978-1-55339-129-6

Canada: The State of the Federation 2004, vol. 18, *Municipal-Federal-Provincial Relations in Canada*, Robert Young and Christian Leuprecht (eds.), 2006
Paper ISBN 1-55339-015-6 Cloth ISBN 1-55339-016-4

Canadian Fiscal Arrangements: What Works, What Might Work Better, Harvey Lazar (ed.), 2005 Paper ISBN 1-55339-012-1 Cloth ISBN 1-55339-013-X

Canada: The State of the Federation 2003, vol. 17, *Reconfiguring Aboriginal-State Relations*, Michael Murphy (ed.), 2005
Paper ISBN 1-55339-010-5 Cloth ISBN 1-55339-011-3

Canada: The State of the Federation 2002, vol. 16, *Reconsidering the Institutions of Canadian Federalism*, J. Peter Meekison, Hamish Telford and Harvey Lazar (eds.), 2004 Paper ISBN 1-55339-009-1 Cloth ISBN 1-55339-008-3

Federalism and Labour Market Policy: Comparing Different Governance and Employment Strategies, Alain Noël (ed.), 2004
Paper ISBN 1-55339-006-7 Cloth ISBN 1-55339-007-5

The Impact of Global and Regional Integration on Federal Systems: A Comparative Analysis, Harvey Lazar, Hamish Telford and Ronald L. Watts (eds.), 2003
Paper ISBN 1-55339-002-4 Cloth ISBN 1-55339-003-2

Canada: The State of the Federation 2001, vol. 15, *Canadian Political Culture(s) in Transition*, Hamish Telford and Harvey Lazar (eds.), 2002
Paper ISBN 0-88911-863-9 Cloth ISBN 0-88911-851-5

Federalism, Democracy and Disability Policy in Canada, Alan Puttee (ed.), 2002
Paper ISBN 0-88911-855-8 Cloth ISBN 1-55339-001-6, ISBN 0-88911-845-0 (set)

Comparaison des régimes fédéraux, 2ᵉ éd., Ronald L. Watts, 2002
Paper ISBN 1-55339-005-9

John Deutsch Institute for the Study of Economic Policy

The 2006 Federal Budget: Rethinking Fiscal Priorities, Charles M. Beach, Michael Smart and Thomas A. Wilson (eds.), 2007
Paper ISBN 978-1-55339-125-8 Cloth ISBN 978-1-55339-126-6

Health Services Restructuring in Canada: New Evidence and New Directions, Charles M. Beach, Richard P. Chaykowksi, Sam Shortt, France St-Hilaire and Arthur Sweetman (eds.), 2006
Paper ISBN 978-1-55339-076-3 Cloth ISBN 978-1-55339-075-6

A Challenge for Higher Education in Ontario, Charles M. Beach (ed.), 2005
Paper ISBN 1-55339-074-1 Cloth ISBN 1-55339-073-3

Current Directions in Financial Regulation, Frank Milne and Edwin H. Neave (eds.), Policy Forum Series no. 40, 2005
Paper ISBN 1-55339-072-5 Cloth ISBN 1-55339-071-7

Higher Education in Canada, Charles M. Beach, Robin W. Boadway and R. Marvin McInnis (eds.), 2005   Paper ISBN 1-55339-070-9 Cloth ISBN 1-55339-069-5

Financial Services and Public Policy, Christopher Waddell (ed.), 2004
Paper ISBN 1-55339-068-7 Cloth ISBN 1-55339-067-9

The 2003 Federal Budget: Conflicting Tensions, Charles M. Beach and Thomas A. Wilson (eds.), Policy Forum Series no. 39, 2004
Paper ISBN 0-88911-958-9 Cloth ISBN 0-88911-956-2

Canadian Immigration Policy for the 21st Century, Charles M. Beach, Alan G. Green and Jeffrey G. Reitz (eds.), 2003
Paper ISBN 0-88911-954-6 Cloth ISBN 0-88911-952-X

Framing Financial Structure in an Information Environment, Thomas J. Courchene and Edwin H. Neave (eds.), Policy Forum Series no. 38, 2003
Paper ISBN 0-88911-950-3 Cloth ISBN 0-88911-948-1

Towards Evidence-Based Policy for Canadian Education/Vers des politiques canadiennes d'éducation fondées sur la recherche, Patrice de Broucker and/et Arthur Sweetman (eds./dirs.), 2002 Paper ISBN 0-88911-946-5 Cloth ISBN 0-88911-944-9

Money, Markets and Mobility: Celebrating the Ideas of Robert A. Mundell, Nobel Laureate in Economic Sciences, Thomas J. Courchene (ed.), 2002
Paper ISBN 0-88911-820-5 Cloth ISBN 0-88911-818-3

Our publications may be purchased at leading bookstores, including the Queen's University Bookstore (http://www.campusbookstore.com/) or can be ordered online from McGill-Queen's University Press, at **http://mqup.mcgill.ca/ordering.php**

For more information about new and backlist titles from Queen's Policy Studies, visit **http://www.queensu.ca/sps/books** or visit the McGill-Queen's University Press web site at: **http://mqup.mcgill.ca/**